The Public Life Of W.f. wallett, The Queen's Jester: An Autobiography Of Forty Years Professional Experience And Travels In The United Kingdom, The United States Of America Including California ......

W.F. Wallett

Nabu Public Domain Reprints:

You are holding a reproduction of an original work published before 1923 that is in the public domain in the United States of America, and possibly other countries. You may freely copy and distribute this work as no entity (individual or corporate) has a copyright on the body of the work. This book may contain prior copyright references, and library stamps (as most of these works were scanned from library copies). These have been scanned and retained as part of the historical artifact.

This book may have occasional imperfections such as missing or blurred pages, poor pictures, errant marks, etc. that were either part of the original artifact, or were introduced by the scanning process. We believe this work is culturally important, and despite the imperfections, have elected to bring it back into print as part of our continuing commitment to the preservation of printed works worldwide. We appreciate your understanding of the imperfections in the preservation process, and hope you enjoy this valuable book.

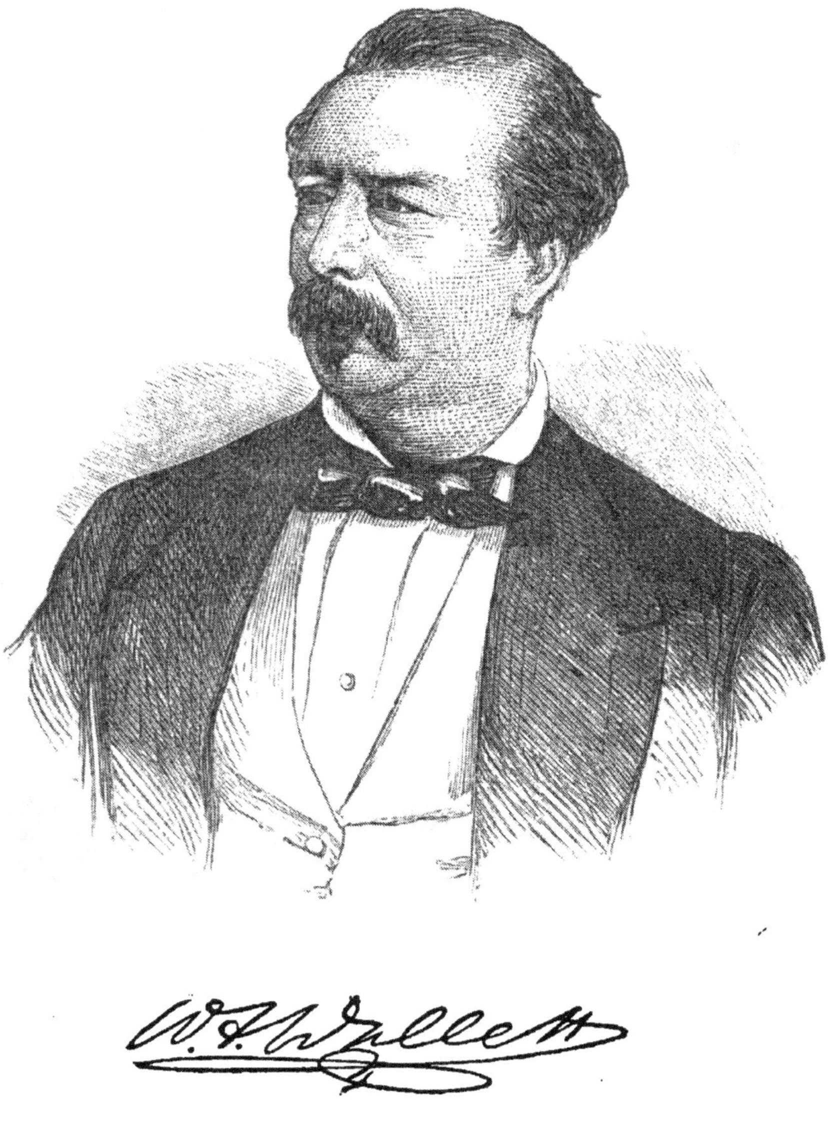

*Henry Frost begs
to present his obt servant
the Author*

THE PUBLIC LIFE

*May 1st
1872.*

OF *Wallett*

W. F. WALLETT,

Carta de Henry

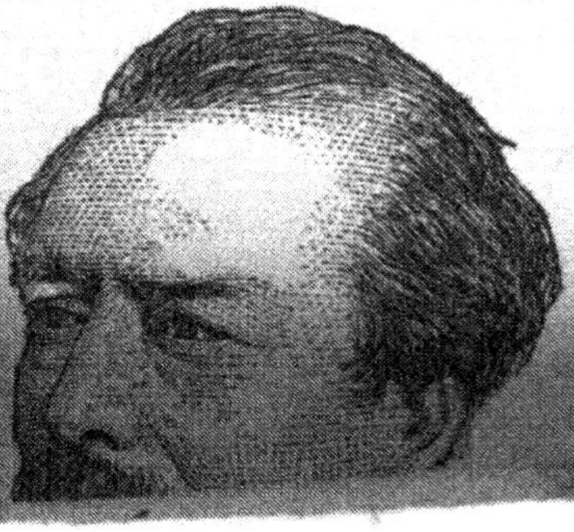

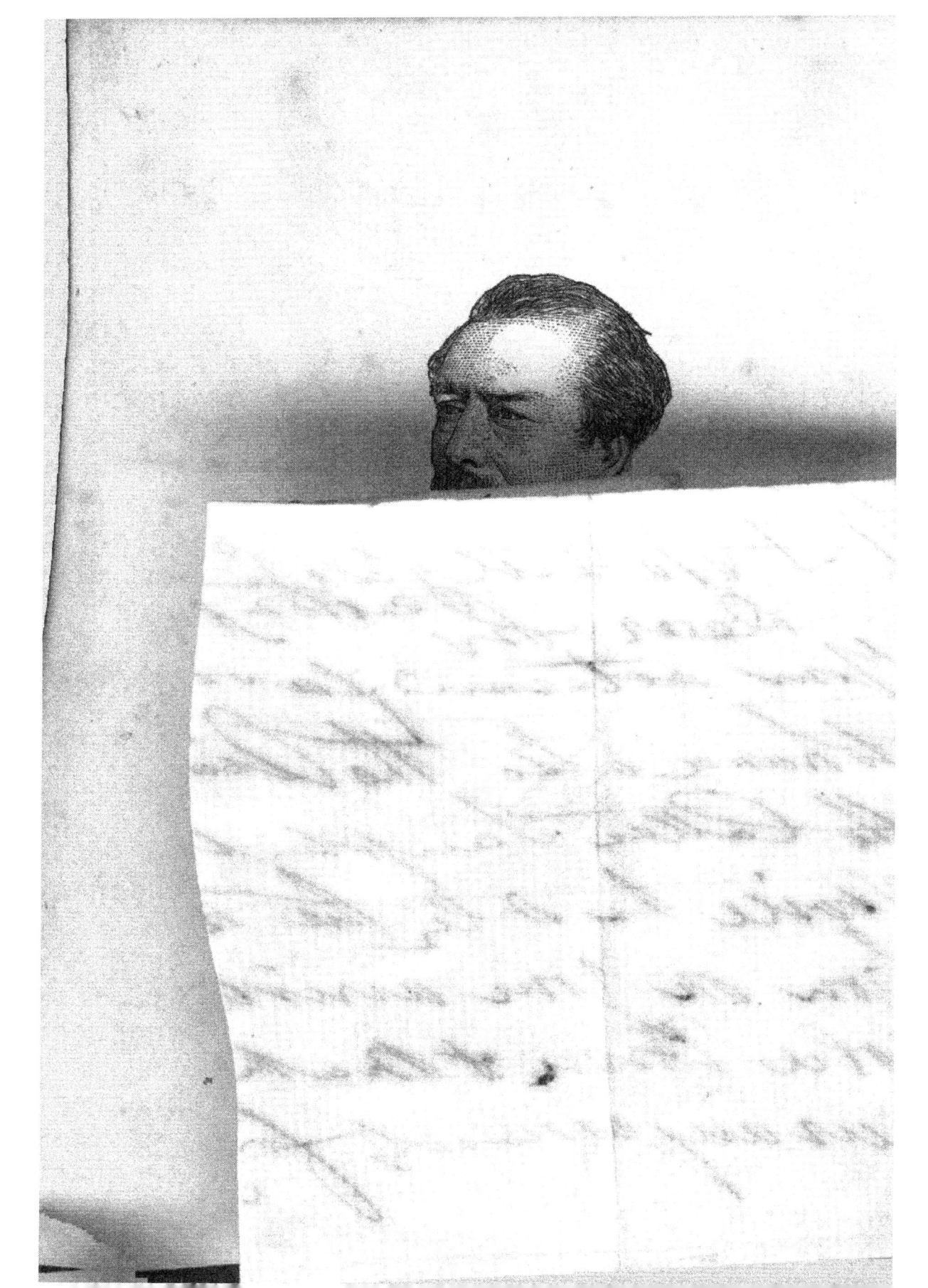

THE PUBLIC LIFE
OF
W. F. WALLETT,

𝕿𝖍𝖊 𝕼𝖚𝖊𝖊𝖓'𝖘 𝕵𝖊𝖘𝖙𝖊𝖗:

AN AUTOBIOGRAPHY

Of Forty Years' Professional Experience and Travels in the United Kingdom, the United States of America (including California), Canada, South America, Mexico, the West Indies, &c.

EDITED BY JOHN LUNTLEY.

THIRD EDITION.

LONDON:
BEMROSE AND SONS, 21, PATERNOSTER ROW; AND DERBY.
THOMAS HAILES LACY, 89, STRAND, W.C.
JOHN MENZIES, 2, S. HANOVER STREET, EDINBURGH.

—

MDCCCLXX.

—

ALL RIGHTS RESERVED.

PREFACE BY THE EDITOR.

WALK up, ladies and gentlemen, and see Wallett, the Queen's jester, the Shakesperian jester—Wallett the scene painter and modelatori—Wallett the posturer—Wallett the manager—Wallett slaying giants and feeding children—Wallett bottling other clowns and putting down the press—Wallett the poet—Wallett the traveller in England, in Ireland, in Scotland, in America, in California, in Mexico, in the West Indies—Wallett writing himself down what he is!

Carried away by our subject we are forgetting the editorial dignity. To proceed in a more proper style :—

There is more than the usual apology for a preface to this work. Mr. Wallett has received many flattering testimonials, to introduce which into his work would be painful to the modesty so conspicuous in his career and in his Autobiography. Two of these are therefore prefixed, and others are added in the appendix. Moreover, the assumption of the title of "Queen's Jester" requires some explanation. Though not regularly patented as Court Jester, it will be seen that Mr. Wallett did act in that capacity, and has been honoured with distinguishing tokens of Her Majesty's approbation. The ancient office of court jester seems to have been merged in the more dignified appointment of poet-laureate. Perhaps some of our sovereigns, particularly the "merry monarch," have thought they could do their own fooling. In his case certainly "majesty" was deprived of its externals according to the old conundrum, and about his time the official jester disappeared from the English court, the last of the race being found in the retinue of the infamous Judge Jeffreys. Our beloved Queen's temporary election, however, has been amply justified by the suffrages of her subjects. For in harmony with the tendency of the age, Mr. Wallett has latterly acted in the spirit of Lord Brougham's altered motto, "Pro rege *lege* grege," and exercised his talents more for the entertainment of the people than for the amusement of royalty.

The very interesting "Book of Days," published by Messrs. Chambers, contains the following remark:—

"It has become the fashion of clowns to circuses to style themselves 'Queen's Jesters'; and there is one of these named Wallett, whose portrait has been engraved among those of the eminent men of the age."

Certainly this fashion was set by Mr. Wallett, who had sufficient warrant for so styling himself, but of course he cannot be accountable for the assumptions of others.

The modern clown or jester is of ancient lineage, and one of the most classical of histrionic characters. His remote ancestors were the mimes of the Greek and Latin stage. Sophron of Syracus, who flourished about 420 B.C. was very celebrated for his mimetic compositions. Plato so much admired his works that he introduced them to Athens, and was accustomed to sleep with them under his pillow. Great celebrity was also attained by some of the Roman mimes who both composed and acted their plays. The names of Laberius and Syrus were conspicuous in the most glorious period of Roman history. Since then a long line of "fools," "gestours," "jounglours," &c. has descended to these days.

The permanence of the character of the jester is not surprising when the usefulness of his functions is considered. "To shoot folly as it flies," and with pointed wit to strike and burst the bubble of the hour, and to do so, evoking the laughter of an audience without causing a pang or a blush, is no mean accomplishment. We need not wonder therefore to find the names and sayings of "fools" carried down the stream of history with those of kings and poets and warriors. One of these waifs is familiar to the readers of the "Edinburgh Review." Though few are aware that its caustic motto by Publius Syrus, "Judex damnatur cum nocens absolvitur," is the sentence of a Roman clown. The editor of Rees's Encyclopædia remarks :—

"We with difficulty can imagine some of the grave and judicious reflections of Syrus to be extracted from the pantomimes which he exhibited on the stage. . . . . The applause given to the pieces of Plautus and Terence did not prevent even the better sort from admiring these pantomimic farces, when enlivened by wit and not debased by indecency. The mimographic poets of the Romans, who chiefly distinguished themselves in these dramatic exhibitions were Sneius Mattius, Decimus Laberius, Publius Syrus, under Julius Cæsar; Philiston, under Augustus; Silo, under Tiberius; Virgilius Romanus, under Trajan; and Marcus Marcellus, under Antoninus. But the most celebrated of all these were Decimus Laberius and Publius Syrus. The first diverted Julius Cæsar so much that he made him a Roman knight, and conferred on him the privilege of wearing gold rings. He had such a wonderful talent at seizing ridicule as to make every one dread his abilities. To this Cicero alludes in writing to Trebutius when he was in Britain with Julius Cæsar, telling him that if he is absent much longer inactive he must be expected to be attacked by the mime Laberius. Publius Syrus, however, gained so much more applause that he retired to Puzzioli, where he consoled himself for his disgrace and the inconstancy of the people and the transient state of human affairs by the following admirable verse :

'Cecidi ego : vadet qui sequitur : laus est publica.'"

A similar sentiment is thus expressed by Dr. Johnson,

"New fashions rise, and different views engage,
Superfluous lags the veteran on the stage."

In our own country the jester was formerly held in considerable esteem. It should be noted, however, that there was generally a distinction between the office of the "jester" and that of the "fool;" the former being deemed honourable, it was frequently filled by an educated gentleman, while the latter was considered menial. One Berdic, "joculator" to William the Conqueror was presented with three towns and five carucates in Gloucestershire. Will Sommers, jester to Henry VIII. was also a man of mark, and his portrait is preserved at Hampton Court. Archie Armstrong, court fool to James I. must have been a great favourite, for that tobacco-hating monarch actually granted him a patent for the manufacture of pipes. And it is even surmised that the prince of all dramatists and poets, Shakspere himself, once fulfilled an engagement as jester. There are four years of his life unaccounted for, unless the clue may be found in a letter addressed in that period by Sir Philip Sidney to his father-in-law, Walsingham. He says, "I wrote to you a letter by Will, my Lord of Leicester's jesting player." Mr. Bruce, in the first volume of the Shakespere Society's papers, asks, "Who was Will?" Besides Shakespere there were only two players of the name known at that time.

As might be expected, the true ideal of a professional

jester is to be found in Shakespere's Yorick, the king's jester, the absence of whose eloquent and loving lips Hamlet mourns when contemplating his skull. "A fellow of infinite jest, of most excellent fancy." And Mr. Wallett has elevated or rather restored in his representation the character of the clown, from that of a coarse buffoon to that of a merry doctor of philosophy. Sometimes attempting the cure of vice and folly after the manner desired by the cynical Jaques :—

> "Invest me in my motley; give me leave
> To speak my mind, and I will through and through
> Cleanse the foul body of the infected world
> If they will patiently receive my medicine."

Sometimes purging out "loathed melancholy" by the exhibition of wholesome mirth. Sometimes brightening even cheerfulness itself by means of

> " Quips and cranks and wanton wiles,
> Nods and becks and wreathed smiles,
> Sport that wrinkled care derides,
> And Laughter holding both his sides."

And at all times infusing the spirit of wisdom in the wine of merriment.

The advantages of the motley suit are very apparent. The sense of the ludicrous is awakened by the eye before it is excited by the ear, and thus the way is prepared for the prosperity of the jest which, as Shakespere says, lies principally "in the ear of him that hears it." Like the wearers of other professional costumes, legal and clerical, jesters are privileged to say and do many things which would not be kindly received from laymen. And as children require pills to be gilded and medicine to be sweetened, so many a salutary but unpalatable lesson may be best administered in the guise of a joke. These things considered, it may be doubted whether the proportion of folly is not greater in the wearers of sober suits than in those disguised as clowns and fools.

The first place among the eulogies of our jester must be given to the following sonnet by a true poet:—

> "Full oft thy efforts in the mimic art
>   I've watched; and marvelled at those facile powers,
>   That through the bright and swiftly gliding hours,
> Such jest and mirth to thousands could impart.
> In truth, I scarcely know what is thy part:
>   Whether to play the Fool in sparkling showers
>   Of jest, or in this sinning world of ours
> With sterling wisdom to amend the heart.
> But this I know, thy genial wit for me
>   Hath stirred life's pulses, beating weak and slow,
>   And chased the heavy shadows from my brow,
> And lit my languid eye with healthful glee.
> And so I pray thy gifts may long remain
> To gladden future days, and banish care and pain."

Another congenial spirit, the late lamented Albert Smith, penned the following alliterative acrostic:—

> "WALLETT, wonder-working wit, with thy wealth of waggery,
> Freshly flung from fun-fraught founts, from thy face fate's frownings flee;
> With thy wedded wit and wisdom, woe's wan wrinkles wane away;
> At thine apt and arch allusions—antidotes to care's array—
> Laughter-loving lieges listen, loudly lauding laughter's lord.
> Long, long live then, lightly lifting melancholy's load abhorr'd;
> Ever eloquent-enchanting, ever ENNUI's enemy;
> Thrilling, thralling, thronging thousands with gay trick and travesty.
> Throned in triumph, motley mentor, Minerva, Momus, meet in thee."

"A merry heart doeth good like medicine," and is generally the offspring of benevolence, seeking to diffuse the happiness it enjoys. The veteran jester, here self-pourtrayed, is an eminent example of this rule and of the reward of the unselfish. "Love, honour, reverence, and troops of friends" are his, and his many charities may cover the imperfections his enemies would discover.

It will readily be believed that our task has been easy and agreeable. Thousands can testify of our dictator, that

> "A merrier man, within the limits of becoming mirth,
> I never passed an hour's talk withal."

In conclusion, we can only wish that you may have as much pleasure in reading, as we have had in "taking the life" of the Queen's Jester.

INTRODUCTION.

"RUDE am I in speech and manner, and ne'er till now stood I in such a presence."

After this humble acknowledgment, permit me in all sincerity to confess that this book has not the slightest pretension to literary excellence. It is merely a disjointed collection of circumstances adventures and accidents, not woven together by that peculiar machinery called "a plot." A mere series of tales forming a tale, which does not exactly come under Shakespere's description, "a round, unvarnished tale." It is not a "round" tale, being really true, it may considered "on the square." No time has been spent in softening down its asperities, or filing off the rough angles of perfect truth. But the latter portion of the Shakesperian quotation is carried out to the letter. For it would have been a great waste of time and valuable material to attempt to varnish or polish such a rough combination of crude facts and observations.

Instead of being entitled "An Autobiography," I think it might, with equal propriety, have been called a collection of reminiscences of the men and manners of my time. My story is a sort of mirror, reflecting the scenes in which I have figured, or, as I might humbly say in the words of the immortal Cæsar narrating his wars, "of which I was a great part."

Having thus explained the quality and object of the work, I shall conclude with a paraphrase of the words of Brutus, "Read me for my cause, and be attentive that you may read."

Spring Villa, Beeston, Notts.,
    All Fools' Day, 1st April, 1870.

CONTENTS.

CHAPTER I.—Page 1 to 9.

Start in life.—First engagements end in grief.—Dispensing sweets.—Advertising in churchyard.—Saved by pigs.—Achieving greatness.—Sympathy.—Retribution for unfeeling husband.—Timely song.—Unlucky voyage.

CHAPTER II.—Page 10 to 15.

Gainsborough mart.—Epitaph on a manager.—Hard times.—Tailoring and boot-making.—Trip to Doncaster.—Bad luck.—Close of an engagement.

CHAPTER III.—Page 16 to 54.

Jemmy Wild's establishment.—Raising the wind.—Coming out strong.—Posturing.—Man monkey.—Accident and fright.—Engagement with Smedley.—Journey to Pontefract.—Suspected tragedian.—Day after the fair.—Decorating a carriage.—Engagement with Thorne.—Doing the statues.—Peripatetic hotel.—Upsetting the cart.—Feeding the dragon.—Ducrow and the knife grinders.—Drama of Napoleon.—Gagging for a benefit.—Successful disappointment.—Restive donkey.—Opinion of dupes.—Courageous manager.—Wakefield.—Dewsbury.—Bradford, flood in dressing room, Christmas Waits.—Careless manager.—Patronage of the vicar.—Hull fair, success stopped.—Attacked by Paddy.—Wooden actors.—Up goes the dinner.—Generous patron.—Escape from explosion.—Leaving the booths.

CHAPTER IV.—Page 55 to 84.

Challenges.—Turning the bridge.—Variety.—Temptation and restitution.—Choking a tale-bearer.—Cooke's company.—Engagement with Van Amburgh.—Rook pie.—Infuriated father.—Forcible ejectment at Tunbridge Wells.—Royal patronage at Windsor.—Cambridge students and Vice-Chancellor.—Carriage building.—Accident to a rider.—Getting into trouble.—Quarrel with Batty.—Fishing at Oxford.—Electioneering speech.—Sudden deaths at Wakefield and Leeds.—Impromptu orchestra.—Upsetting a throne.—Superseding Barry.—Saturday night at Birmingham.—Christmas rehearsal.—Settling with Batty.

CHAPTER V.—Page 85 to 94.

Soda-water making.—Starting a circus.—Yarmouth bloaters.—Bad luck at Colchester and Leicester.—Great business at Nottingham.—Bradford, testimonial.—Limbs locked at Huddersfield.—Cholera at Wigan—Selling off at Salford.—Winding up.

CHAPTER VI.—Page 95 to 113.

Leaving for America.—Greeting at New York.—First performance.—Triumph at Philadelphia.—Boston.—Baltimore.—New York again.—Disputed contract.—Killing the Giants—Travels in Canada.—Floating circus on the Mississipi.—All aboard.—Fraternizing with Rice.—Return *via* Cuba.—Hot and cold passage.—Home to Frankfort.—Tour in Indiana.—Row with managers.—Mississippi again.—Frightening the Negroes.

CHAPTER VII.—Page 114 to 122.

Back to England.—Honourable settlement and presentation.—Join Pablo.—Irish Chinaman.—Success at Glasgow.—Presentation at Birmingham.—Christmas journey to London.—Compliment at Liverpool.—Sudden start for America.—Second reception at New York.—Benefit at Philadelphia.

CHAPTER VIII.—Page 123 to 139.

Embark for California.—Rough voyage.—Panama.—Man overboard.—Coast of Mexico.—Steamboat drill.—Arrival at San Francisco.—Kean Buchanan.—Doings at the gold diggings.—Robbery and murder.—Eye lotion.—Trapped in a bear-pit.—Giant trees.—Chinese dramatics.—A converted Friend.

CHAPTER IX.—Page 140 to 152.

Return to England.—Selling the landlord.—Opening of Park at Hull.—Feasting children.—Fatal accident to Wolfenden.—Classic circus at Birmingham.—Unclothing clothier at Wakefield.—Appearance at Drury Lane.—The male syren.

CHAPTER X.—Page 153 to 161.

Criticizing the critics.—Reception at Edinburgh.—Dundee.—Too popular.—Serious illness.—Whiskey cure.—Gustavus Brooke.—Voyage to America.

CHAPTER XI.—Page 161 to 171.

Reception at Philadelphia.—Escape from Shipwreck at Hull.—Escape from railway accident at Rugby.—Escape from boiler explosion at New Orleans.—Recovery of baggage.—Christy Minstrels.—Presentation at Philadelphia.—Voyage back to England.—Engagement at Huddersfield.—Recognition at Holmfirth.—Presentation at Huddersfield.

CHAPTER XII.—Page 172 to 180.

Taking stock of fellow passengers.—Sick lady.—Lieut. Thompson.—Charitable concert.—Discovery of ignorance.—Taught by a sweep.—Saturday night at sea.—Sunday on board.—The captain posed.—The bishop at sea.—Interrupted sermon.—Dropping the anchor.

APPENDIX.

Page 181 to 188.

THE LIFE OF WALLETT.

CHAPTER I.

"All the world's a stage,
And all the men and women merely players,
They have . . . their entrances."—*As You Like It.*

MY name is Wallett. This is my real name; for I am not ashamed of my profession, and never cared to follow it in the disguise of an *alias*. So I have carried my Wallett for forty years through many lands—a Rosicrucian pilgrim, a missionary of sweetness and light and heart-easing mirth.

Wisdom, now-a-days, does not always cry in the streets; nor wit either. Punch is not content with his peripatetic pulpit, but addresses a larger circle from the platform of the press. So I step out of the ring, to present my friends with a printed wallet of wit, wisdom, and wayfaring. It is a motley production, but the colours are generally bright, and ancient writers do report that "variety is pleasing."

It is now forty years ago since I made my first appearance before the footlights of the Theatre Royal at Hull, my native town. It was in a subordinate part, my duty being to bring in the waters at the opening of a sea scene. As in youth, so through life, I never took kindly to water. There were several other artists engaged in the same occupation. They were a set of forward young fellows, but my innate modesty keeping me in the back-ground, I was crushed by the advancing ship. This instantly brought me to the surface, when I walked rapidly over the waves for the nearest port of safety, but unfortunately fell among the breakers. The stage manager and prompter fell upon me with cudgels, and did for me what I have often done since, cudgelled my brains, and nearly broke every bone in my body. Thus ended my first engagement.

Not desiring more of this treatment, seeing no chance on the stage, and discouraged by my first sea voyage, I thought a change of scene might be more in accordance with my views. I therefore made my way to a small building known as the Summer Theatre, then being fitted up for a company under the management of Mr. Samuel Butler, the tragedian. Here I obtained an engagement as an assistant artist. I have no doubt I should have made rapid strides in my new profession, but for another of my mishaps. Modesty again barred my preferment, for I kept myself in the rear, by devoting most of my time to the grinding of colours, though I occasionally had some of the primest part of the work to do in priming the canvas. At this juncture a circus company arrived in the town, headed by the Great Ducrow. I went to see them, and this was my first visit to any circus. Ducrow gave his original and wonderful delineation of a Life on the Ocean Wave, quite different to my previous experience of that life. As a scaffold, at the Summer Theatre, we used two 36-ft. ladders, placed horizontally from the boxes to the stage, forming a platform on which the artists stood to decorate the boxes. There was only one support in the centre. While the artists were at dinner, I removed this support, which gave a wonderful elasticity to the ladders, on which, in humble imitation of Ducrow, I appeared as the Shipwrecked Mariner. My improvised horse had a lofty swinging and bounding pace, which greatly delighted me, but one unlucky extra bound of my wooden steed precipitated me into the pit below. I had broken the ladder, which broke my horse's back, broke his gallop, nearly broke my neck, and actually broke my engagement as a scenic artist.

My dear and early friend, Lysander Steel Thompson, admiring my talent and energy, and sympathizing with my misfortunes, recommended me to Mr. William Abbott, of the Theatre Royal, Crowle, where I had the honour of being enrolled as a member of the legitimate dramatic corps. The theatre was the club room of the George and Dragon Inn. The stage was on a level with the auditorium. The noble ceiling was at least seven feet in the clear above it; but the hanging scenery, though rolled up in the neatest manner, made a deduction of eighteen inches from the original altitude. Mr. Thompson, my kind-hearted patron, as long Tom Coffin, made his debût on the same night as I did. Now this star of the night was six feet one inch in his stocking-feet, which unfortunate longitude prevented his walking from back to front of the stage without ducking his head under the scenes. The worthy manager and his amiable wife were very poor, but very honest, and truly indefatigable in their endeavours to bring up a large family. They even printed their own bills, which the actors delivered. Among other modes of raising the wind, the manageress and leading actress employed some of her leisure time in the manufacture of sweetmeats for the habitués of the saloon. When I first went, the house was but thinly attended, notwithstanding the attraction of the star, and the impression my first appearance should have made. To the best of my recollection there were about six in the gallery, four in the pit, and on the front chairs, dignified by the title of boxes, sat one, "alone in his glory." I did not appear in the first piece, but had to prepare myself for an interlude. My part was then to take round a basket of the aforesaid sweetmeats to the audience. Here I met with a mortifying rebuff; for I was severely snubbed on my first application. With the basket on my arm and a smile on my face, I in the blandest manner addressed the solitary one on the reserved seats—"Will you purchase any humbugs,* sir?" To which he replied, "Certainly not—humbugged enough by the performance." This unkindness nearly broke my heart, and brought to a sudden close another act of my life; but I concluded it was owing to my neglect of Shakespere's maxim, "Sweets to the sweet."

My next appearance was as a distributor of bills, in which character I came to grief as before. It was about the eighth week of the company's stay in this small town. The novelty of the entertainment had worn off, and the audience, not large at first, had grown small by degrees and beautifully less; in fact, they became conspicuous by

---

* Yorkshire for brandy balls.

their absence. In this state of affairs, I perpetrated what in the thoughtlessness of youth, I considered a good joke, but of which I have repented ever since. In my rounds as an advertising medium, I adopted the following expedient. I procured a number of sticks, sharpened at one end and slit at the other, like those used by butter merchants to display their tickets of "Prime Dorset, Rich Cheshire," &c. I carefully folded up my bills, and having inserted one in each cleft stick, I very improperly stuck them in different parts of the churchyard. The vicar came down in great displeasure; though a good friend of ours, he could not overlook such an outrage. Being one of the Great Unpaid, he summoned me to attend before him, and desired me to make an ample apology. As I look at it now, I fear I only aggravated my offence by my defence. I told him my reason for the act complained of was, that as I had been distributing bills for some time, and none of their living recipients had responded, I was determined to extend the invitation to the occupants of the low green hillocks. The excellent vicar, after showing me the impropriety of my conduct, was pleased to pardon the apparent sacrilege.

Though the theatre was thus deserted, yet we were not, for we were surrounded by troops of friends. It was winter, and pig-killing time. Then came our salvation. Pigs to the rescue! Though poor, we were much respected by the farmers round, more so by their wives, and still more by their pretty innocent daughters. So it fell out, no sooner had each particular pig parted with its vitality, than each member of the company received his quota of sausage, pork pie, and pig's fry. In fact, it seemed as if we had a vested interest in each individual of the swinish multitude in that locality. Things went on thus swimmingly for a time. Though money was scarce, a four-bushel sack of potatoes, borne on the brawny back of a farmer's man, was considered by the manageress and money-taker a fair equivalent for the admission of the bearer and two friends to a front seat in the gallery. Our transactions in kind became so notorious, that a canal sailor, who during our stay made a voyage to London and back, inquired of a friend on his return, "Are the players not gone yet?" He received the reply, "No, and they never will go while there's a pig left to squeak in the parish." At length this last squeak came, and we went. To those of our kind providers who survive, I tender my hearty thanks for their fostering care during these early struggles.

We sailed from Crowle, with many parting cheers, in a vessel called the Mary Ann, bound for Barrow-on-the-Humber. We carried with us the good will of all, and a letter of introduction from the worthy vicar to the rector of Barrow. We were hospitably received by him, and established in his barn, which we distinguished by the style of Theatre. It was here that the tide in the affairs of men took a favourable turn for me. It happened thus. I lodged with a newly married couple in a humble cot, and the wife was in an interesting condition. In the middle of the night I heard the cry of travail. It was several times repeated, but answered by a coarse "Lie still, you'll be better in the morning." I became excited, and could bear to hear no more. So I ran down stairs and out of doors without shoes or hat, and found, to my astonishment, a reception in a bed of snow a foot in depth. Nothing daunted, I ran half a mile to the village doctor. After knocking loudly and often at his door, the doctor called out "Who's there?" Having made known my business, he considerately allowed me to remain bare-footed and bare-headed in the snow, while he deliberately dressed. My turn then came; for he no sooner stepped into the snow, than I took him by the nether garment and coat collar, and propelled him up the street at a pace surprising to himself and lowering to the dignity of his profession. On arriving at the house there was a busy scene. A roaring fire, and an assembly of a dozen matrons, who had a kettle boiling, and made me a cup of hot tea. They chafed my benumbed limbs, and rewarded me with a thousand blessings. I had the pleasure of hearing that the event was soon over, and the mother "doing as well as could be expected." From this moment I was the hero of Barrow. I went to bed obscure, and woke up famous. The inhabitants became interested in the welfare of our company. The season was a success, and on my benefit night the ladies rallied round me, gave me a bumping house and several handsome presents. For the first time in my life I was the happy possessor of five pounds.

Before we left Barrow, an incident occurred which looked very like retribution. The unsympathizing husband referred to, was in the habit of poaching, and had a fowling-piece, the barrel of which was shortened to conceal it under his topcoat. On the morning before our departure, this man was out on one of his illegal expeditions. He had placed a cork in the muzzle of his gun to keep out the snow. The gun being hidden beneath his coat with the muzzle immediately under his armpit; by some means the trigger was caught, and the gun went off. The cork and charge lodged in his shoulder, wounding it in a frightful manner, and rendering amputation necessary. They brought him home, and, as he shrieked with pain, unkind though it was, I could not help repeating, "Lie still, you'll be better in the morning."

Our next scene of operations was Market Rasen, in Lincolnshire, where we were invited to assist in the festivities to celebrate the coronation of his Majesty King William IV. I had the honour of dining with the *élite* of the neighbourhood, at the Greyhound Hotel. By a slice of luck, I had received from a friend in London an early copy of a new song, "Here's a health to the King, God bless him." After the cloth was removed, and when harmony reigned, I had the pleasure of introducing this song, which was several times encored. My use of this opportunity gained for me the favour of the best families of the place, and was another stepping-stone in my career. I had a bumping benefit, and was thus enabled to send my excellent mother five pounds, in token of my gratitude for her early care and teaching.

Our theatre was a barn at the back of the Greyhound, and is still observable from the Manchester, Sheffield, and Lincolnshire Railway.

It was at this time I had an opportunity of displaying my pugilistic talent. I remember well, it was on the Saturday morning I received a letter from my dear mother, informing me of her ill health, so I resolved to start for home at the conclusion of the night's entertainment. There were no railways then, no powerful steamboats to cross the Humber.

I walked all night, and arrived at New Holland early on Sunday morning. There was but one house there then, and the mode of crossing the river was by a large open boat called a lugger. I was the only passenger to go, and the weather was cold and boisterous. So the captain and mate, who formed the entire crew, held a consultation and determined that it was not worth while to make the passage. This was very discouraging after my long journey in the dark, and being then in sight of my mother's home. My entreaties and tears, backed by the offer of five shillings, at length induced the mercenaries to set sail. The weather had now become more stormy, and when we gained mid-channel it had attained the proportions of a gale. The crew had another conference, when they decided to put back to New Holland. Persuasion was in vain, prayers unheeded, about she came on her return voyage. On landing they refused to return my money, adding insult to injury, and threatening violence. The altercation soon collected a small crowd, who hearing my case and sympathizing with myself and sick parent, took the part of the stranger. Emboldened by their support, I more peremptorily demanded my money back, which being as firmly refused, my friends advised a process signified by "Take it out of him." Nothing loth, no sooner said than done. Opposed by youth and a good cause, the blustering skipper was laid on his beam ends. Then fearing a rough handling from the spectators, who all seemed to desire that the mate should share the punishment as he shared in the dirty transaction, the money was reluctantly returned to me. I then retraced my steps to Market Rasen, where I arrived fatigued in body and disappointed in mind, about 9.30 p.m., with the object of my pious pilgrimage unaccomplished.

CHAPTER II.

"I am ambitious for a motley coat."—*As You Like It.*

AFTER remaining some time a member of Mr. Abbott's company, I began to desire a change; and having heard much of the wonders and attractions of Gainsborough Mart, I resolved to visit that noted fair. After a long trudge my labours were amply rewarded by my first view of Wombwell's Menagerie, while my ears were regaled by the sweet harmony of the powerful and talented band. Those who can remember this orchestra can imagine the impression it made upon me when the Hallelujah Chorus first struck my ear. Next to them was announced in large letters "Milton's, late Adam's Grand Circus." Milton was a groom, and had by some "hocus pocus" obtained his late master's property; and Mr. Henry Adams, father of the present Mr. Charles Adams, had joined Ducrow at Astley's, and was the only real rival that great artist ever had. Little Jemmy Scott's Coronation Pavilion was also there. This was the most magnificent show that travelled at that time, far surpassing Richardson in his glory. And by a singular coincidence this proprietor too was a myth; for a person of the name of Charley Yeoman had contrived to oust him, and had taken full possession *à la* Milton. It was at this establishment I obtained a fresh engagement, and here I first donned the motley. My part combined the clown of the outside parade and the assistant scene-painter within.

I took a lodging at a beerhouse in the Mart Yard, the first house licensed in the provinces under the New Beer Act. I called at the house four or five years ago, and found it still occupied by the original landlady. Here again I had a reverse and a return of my former ill luck. Having had a difference with the manager, who fined me for some supposed neglect, I determined to give him a Roland for his Oliver. In the course of the next week I had to rub in a sketch of a country churchyard, the scene being designed for a new drama entitled "Presumptive Evidence." Out of revenge I wrote upon one of the principal tombstones in the foreground :—

> "To the memory of Charley Yeoman,
> Trombone player and showman,
> Who died respected by no man."

Of course this epitaph caused my immediate discharge. Poor fellow, the joke was too grave. Two months after he died a victim to cholera.

I was once more cast adrift on the world. So with a light heart and empty wallet I made my way to Tickhill, Yorkshire, known over the country side as "Tickhill-God-help-me-where-all-the-poor-creatures-come-from." Here I found my old friend and manager, Mr. Abbott, who again received me with a warm welcome. But as you may guess from the name of the town, business was far from prosperous. In fact, before the end of the season we were reduced to starvation point. There I became companion and shared bed and crust with a brother of a late lamented judge, who was acting under the name of Belgrave. We were driven to extremities when another farmer proved a friend in need. He sent us a piece of home-fed bacon, which was hailed with rapture. We did not eat it, it was far too valuable. It was placed in a three-legged iron pot, from which it was never removed. Any vegetables we could obtain were added from day to day, so our stock pot never failed, neither was the bacon sensibly diminished.

By this time the gloss had worn off our apparel, and we presented what is called a "seedy" appearance. Just then my friend Belgrave received a large parcel from London, containing blue broad cloth sufficient for a suit of clothes, and an old-fashioned silver watch, an heir-loom apparently by its antique look, round as a turnip, with black hands and a very dirty face. Watches of the same class may be bought in Tottenham Court Road by the bushel. There was the cloth, but how was it to be made up, and where were the trimmings to be got? which in those days would cost as much as an entire suit does now, cloth included. Necessity proved the mother of invention, so I suggested the possibility of finding a tailor who would make the clothes, and take the watch in payment. This was soon arranged, and the suit was made. A hat was forthcoming; but what about the boots to match? For his only pair was in a deplorable state. It happened during my employment as artist to the establishment, that I had to mount to a beam of the barn to adjust the scenery. There I met with a treasure-trove in the shape of a large pair of leather hedging mittens, with gauntlet tops thick enough for soles. Delighted with the discovery, I rushed home to my companion shouting, *Eureka!* By means of a broken fork and some taching ends that I begged from a benevolent cobbler, I soled my friend's boots. This occured two days before the St. Leger at Doncaster. I had no new suit; but with the assistance of a pound of logwood and alum in proportion, I managed to give my slate coloured clothes somewhat of a healthy and natural complexion. My hat had assumed chameleon hues, like hats at watering places which have suffered a sea change, and vary their colours with every movement of their wearers' heads. By a process known among the Jews as "clobbering," I restored the old hat to almost its pristine beauty. It really looked well. Even Davy Hewitt, my old friend and brother actor, might have been proud of its wonderful restoration. We were now equipped for our trip to Doncaster. It was a lovely morning when we started, but we had scarcely proceeded three miles before the rain began to decend in earnest. Umbrellas we had none, so we were exposed to the pitiless storm. I left Tickhill gloveless, but the action of the rain upon my dyed garments soon furnished me with blue gloves, tipped with purple. My white shirt became an odd spectacle, being adorned with all manner of grotesque figures of strange colours like those on the dresses of the Chinese. My face assumed a colour from which my eyes had a blue look-out. Poor Belgrave laughed heartily at my transformation. His mirth however was soon checked. The leather with which I had soled his boots, though thick, was soft and porous, and through tramping in the mud, had become saturated. While travelling over the soft roads no particular inconvenience resulted; but oh, how different on the paving stones at the entrance of Doncaster! His sodden soles adhered to the pavement like the suckers used by boys, so that he found it impossible to move without leaving his soles behind. There he stood, and still it rained. Then I laughed; for it was my innings now. There was but one remedy for this fix—to remove the soles upon which I had expended so much time and ingenuity. But how? A knife was wanted, and we tried in vain to borrow one. The bystanders, greatly amused by my absurd figure and the strange position of my companion, replied to our entreaties for the loan of a knife by asking whether we wanted to commit suicide. At last one was procured, and the soles were removed, but so hastily that the in-soles were carried away with them, which converted the boots into gaiters. Thus released, we left the soles and our tormentors behind. In the action of walking, every side of the boot gaiters came in succession to the front. By an unfrequented road we made for the Thorne and Doncaster Canal; where we expected to meet Captain Barker of the "Speedwell," packet, a friend and amateur theatrical, from whom we were sure to receive a hearty and hospitable welcome.

But, my luck again! instead of Captain Barker we found on board a temporary captain, a stranger, our friend being detained by illness at Thorne. Our last hope was gone; so being without money or friends, we had to return to Tickhill, not having tasted food since five in the morning. We had walked twenty-five miles through the storm, with (not upon) empty stomachs, and our larder at home could afford us but slight refreshment. At Tickhill once more, our poverty well qualified us to claim the citizenship of that City of Destitution.

My connection with the Abbotts terminated soon after this. Their memory will be ever green, being endeared by many acts of kindness. I was shocked to hear of the sudden close of their lives. After enduring toil and privation many years, they emigrated to St. Louis, to join a son settled there in affluence. Soon after landing, they, their son, daughter, and grandchildren were all carried off by the awful visitation of cholera.

CHAPTER III.

"One man in his time plays many parts."—As You Like It.

BIDDING farewell to my companion, Belgrave, in the hope of a future meeting, which was never realized in consequence of his early death, I started for Leeds. There I joined a theatrical booth belonging to Mr. Wild, better known as "Old Jemmy." This concern was a sort of amphitheatre, being made up of a fortune-telling pony, a tight-rope dancer, and a slight theatrical entertainment. A very severe winter was just over, and matters were not then very brilliant, yet I received a warm reception. I instantly set to work to remodel the establishment, and get it in order for the coming fairs. Towards the end of the first week, the band, consisting of the manager, his three sons, and myself promoted to the rank of drum major, promenaded the district, to acquaint His Majesty's lieges of the great and intellectual treat in store for them at the moderate charge of threepence. Though very poor I was always proud, though not of my poverty. The day was very cold, with a sharp easterly wind. My outward man was not well protected by pilot cloth or fur; nor the inner man well fortified to resist the relentless foe. I endeavoured to conceal my manifest toes in the snow from the observation of the girls, while beating my drum. The manager, a very old man with a loud voice, persisted in announcing the performance in the intervals of the music. The piece to be performed was "The Floating Beacon," which he proclaimed as follows :—" This evening will be represented a drama called The Floating *Bacon*," to which a wag replied, in the Yorkshire dialect, "and a very good thing too, Jemmy, wi' a bit of cabbage to it." The farce for the evening was "Raising the Wind," rather an ominous title, for a storm came on after the conclusion of the performance. At four in the morning, I and others were called up to disentangle the wrecked theatre of its sails and tackle. The canvas roof, and the new scenery I had painted, were torn to rags. While sitting upon the ridge-pole of the demolished roof, clearing the *débris*, the factory bells rang out the hour for work. Then hundreds of the work people passed by, and many stopped to look at the ruin. I believe I gave vent to my feelings in emphatic language, for a small urchin called out, "Eh, Mr. Wallett, don't grumble, ye were raising the wind yourselves last night." Our booth however was somewhat dilapidated before, and the rain coming through the roof rendered it impossible to keep the violins in tune. On one occasion, the leader of the orchestra, a talented but eccentric character, called Dr. Down, hearing the manager's daughter sing, "Buy a Broom," stopped playing and looked up, exclaiming, "Better tell your father to buy a new tilt to the roof."

We soon recovered from our disaster, owing to the happy disposition of Mr. Wild and the industry of his three sons, backed by my judgment and energy, and all encouraged by Mrs. Wild; and the establishment became one of the most prosperous in the country. In the next spring we turned out with new equipage, and all outward and visible signs of improvement. I became over-exalted with pride, which was on one occasion very properly rebuked. On the opening day of the renovated establishment, when standing on the top of the steps in gorgeous apparel, displaying almost as many glories and all the vanity of the peacock, as some little boys were climbing the steps, I called out to one, "Get down, you young rascal." He looked me steadily in the face, and replied, "Oh, oh, 'get down young rascal!' when you were here last winter, with no top to your show, you said 'Walk up, ladies and gentlemen!'"

During my stay at Gainsborough Mart, I observed a very clever young man, a posturer advertised as "the Chinese Nondescript," whose real name was William Cole. His performance was so attractive that I resolved to acquire the practice. I did so to great perfection while belonging to Mr. Wild's company, which added much to my popularity and my pocket. In fact I became so celebrated in this line, that at Bingley, Keighley, and Skipton I sometimes had four or five surgeons on the stage to witness my art. It was considered marvellous at the time, though common enough now. This new acquirement introduced me to another branch of the show trade, namely, playing the man-monkey. An interruption occurred on my first appearance in this character in "Jack Robinson and his Monkey." This was at Bradford. The leader of the band, either inebriate or inattentive, played the wrong piece of music at a very tragical moment. I was about to die when he played a lively air. So I stepped down to the footlights, and looking him in the face, asked aloud, "Do you think any monkey in the world could die to such music as that?"

My second appearance as monkey had an unfortunate conclusion. Just at the close of the drama, the property man, Jem Farrar, was charging a horse pistol, when it exploded in his mouth, shattering his jaws frightfully. I saw him fall, and instantly rushed to his assistance. Seeing his state I took him on my back, and though a heavy man, I carried him to the Dispensary in Darley Street. It was then past eleven o'clock, and the place was closed. I rang at the door, which was opened by a woman with a candle in her hand. Her fright may be imagined when she saw the apparition of a man-monkey with his tail trailing on the ground, and a half-dead man on his back, with the blood streaming down. One glance sufficed. She fell senseless to the ground, and the candle was extinguished. I strode over her in the dark, with my heavy load. Knowing the building well, I ascended the grand staircase, and perceiving a light issuing beneath a door, with one knock I brought out the house surgeon. As he opened the door, and the blaze of gaslight from inside revealed the horrible figures, he too nearly fainted away. A few words convinced him that I was of earthly mould, and he promptly summoned several surgeons. Surrounding the bed of poor Farrar, they had but one opinion, that his case was hopeless. One of them remarked, "We can do nothing for him." Farrar shook his fist at him, being unable to speak. A fine old surgeon, Dr. McTurk, seeing this action, said, "Come, boys, the man has pluck enough to live through any thing. Off coats, boys, and let us do the best we can to save him." They did so. His life was preserved, and I believe he survives to this day.

Shortly after this I quitted the illegitimate drama, posturing, and monkey business, and took an engagement in a legitimate theatrical company, under the management of Mr. Smedley. I made my first appearance as "Killmallock, in "The Mountaineers," at Alford, Lincolnshire. The success of my opening night secured me a lengthened engagement. It was a very respectable troupe, and the manager highly esteemed. Salaries low, but as certain as the light. The season at Alford proving a failure, it was determined to remove to Pontefract, Yorkshire. As we had a week to perform the journey, the manager, in addition to our salaries, allowed us a moderate sum for expenses on the road, to travel in an agreeable manner. The usual way being very circuitous, as I was well acquainted with the direct route, I formed a party of four to undertake the journey on foot. Having sent our luggage with the wardrobe and properties, we started in good health and high spirits, and blooming fortunes. One of our party was Mr. Jones, the leading actor, a ripe scholar and a good tragedian, but a most careless man. He never had anything, but was always wondering where he could get something. Therefore, when we started, we were all surprised to see Jones with something resembling a great drab coat hanging on his arm. Towards noon there came on a heavy storm of rain, when our worthy tragedian ensconced himself in the interior of his drab coat. It was a present from his landlord at Alford, and had apparently been the property of a country post-boy at the beginning of the present century. It was a double-breasted one, and the collar was so high, that it continually pushed off the tragedian's hat. It was like a horse collar. The waist nearly up to his shoulders, and the skirts so long as to oblige him to hold them up out of the mud. A more comical figure it is impossible to imagine. We all had a hearty laugh at him, but, I suspect, having the advantage over us in the comfort of the coat, he was the winning one. Arriving at the Ferry House, Burringham, we found, to our great joy, a large taproom vacant, with a glowing fire, and took undisputed possession. Doffing our upper garments, we surrendered ourselves to warmth and comfort, which we all, except the wearer of the impervious coat, greatly needed. He, snugly planted in the chimney corner, and wrapped in his singular envelope, contemplated our dripping condition with much satisfaction. But his serenity was short-lived. I having borrowed a coat in which to go down to the ferry, to arrange for our crossing the river, discovered a posted bill, headed, "*Stolen*, a Drab Coat," and offering a reward of £1 for information leading to the conviction of the thief. "Oh, Mr. Jones, the tragedian, here's a rod in pickle for you!" thought I. So without more ado, I communicated with the village constable, informing him that such a coat was now on the back of a stranger at the Ferry House Inn, and urging him to come immediately, lest the culprit should escape across the river. No time was lost, the minister of the law almost forestalled my return. My friend was still snug in his warm nook, unsuspecting, though not unsuspected. The constable, with staff in one hand, and a description of the stolen coat in the other, abruptly addressed Jones thus—"Where did you get that coat, my fine fellow?" Jones was amazed, and with knitted brows and flashing eyes, his honest blood crimsoning his forehead to the roots of his hair, replied, "I'll answer no such questions to you, vile caitiff dog." His virtuous indignation was wasted on Dogberry, who, with no gentle touch of his bâton on the shoulder of the drab coat, commanded, in the king's name, the wearer to stand erect, that the coat might be identified; and we were called upon to aid and assist should resistance be offered. Whereupon, we all cried out " Shame," I loudest of all. But explanation, entreaties, threats, and cajolery were unavailing. "Yes, this is the coat—drab coat, high collar, short waist, large buttons—there's no doubt about it, this is the coat, with the thief in it." Matters were looking serious, and I began to repent of my practical joke. So I came forward, and considerately asked what was the distance from where the robbery had been committed. It was within a few hundred yards. "Can the owner of the stolen coat be brought forward to identify it? We had better send for him." All concurred in this suggestion. The owner was fetched. Said the constable, "I have found the coat and the thief," repeating the description. The owner, however, replied, "That is not my coat, though very like it; but mine had pearl buttons." The constable retired, without saying Good day. We all congratulated Jones on his escape. The jolly landlord stood glasses round. The owner, being a needy man, Jones, in gratitude for his release, made him a present of the coat that had brought himself into trouble, wishing him better luck with it.

The weather moderated. We crossed the ferry, and went to Kidby, where, on board his packet, we found the hospitable Captain Barker, whom I and Belgrave missed at Doncaster. He gave us a free passage to Thorne, where a good night's rest and good English fare made us forget the inclement journey, and even Jones had schooled himself to laugh at the misfortune entailed by the coat.

On the road again, a few miles brought us to Newbridge, where, taking the Goole and Leeds canal, we came in a few hours in sight of ancient Pontefract. Our troubles were past; those of the manager were to come. The theatre had been decorated and well advertised to open with a new company for the race week. But on our arrival we found, to the manager's dismay, that we were a day after the fair. The races were on the week before we got there. We opened the theatre, but of course did no business. We could have done as much on the Goodwin Sands, playing to shipwrecked mariners. This town is famous for the growth of liquorice, which is manufactured into a kind of Spanish juice, and forms the "Pomfret cakes." But the manager's mistake made us the greatest cakes Pontefract ever produced.

While with this company I had the honour of making the acquaintance of the following actors who belonged to it. Old Mr. Neville and his daughter, Mr. and Mrs. Lockwood, Mr. and Mrs. Geo. Skerritt, Mr. Fitzroy, and Mr. Whafford.

But again I got into trouble. The manager had a very handsome light omnibus on two wheels for the conveyance of his family. It was modestly painted black, with a light olive green line to enliven it. It was rather too plain for my taste. So as it was standing one day in a yard at the back of the theatre, I caught sight of it through the back door, while touching up a scene, and conceived an idea which I hastened to carry out. Furnished with a straight edge and a pot of chrome yellow, I soon decorated our worthy manager's private carriage by printing in large letters on each side "Smedley's Bread Cart." For this display of my sign-writing talent I received my weekly stipend in neatly folded writing paper, on which was inscribed, "I'll keep my cart, and you'll seek your bread elsewhere."

I next joined Mr. W. S. Thorne, the proprietor of a pavilion in huge proportions built in the form of the Towers of Warsaw. He was in opposition to my old friend Wild. He commenced at Keighley in Yorkshire at the opening of the new market there. Previous to the commencement of the fête, four London acrobats arrived, whose names were Heng, Constantine, Morris, and Whitton. The Constantine of that day was the Henry Boleno of this. This party was engaged by Mr. Wild as a counter attraction to us. Among other entertainments, Constantine represented the Grecian statues, which were then quite new, having been shortly before invented, and introduced by Ducrow, at Astley's. We commenced on Saturday, and the statues were our most formidable rivals; they were exceedingly effective and successful. So much so, that I made up my mind to obtain the dress and properties, which were first-class. So on the Saturday night, after the performances, I introduced myself to Constantine. As the acrobatic troupe had travelled from London, and only received one night's salary, to provide needful supplies for himself and party, he concluded to accept my liberal offer for his costume and the appointments of the statues. On Monday morning the strife between the rival establishments was resumed. Of course I lost no time in making proper arrangements, and advertising the representation of the statues at our establishment that had been so successful at the opposition shop. The plan succeeded; we carried the day. In the height of the professional battle, Mrs. Wild sent for Constantine. "Why, they're doing the statues at the other place, and carrying all before them. Go and get your dress, you must do the statues." "But I cannot," he said. "You must." "Impossible; I've got no dress, no properties." "Why, where are those you had on Saturday night." "I've sold them." "Sold them!" shrieked the worthy manageress, "Sold them! sold them! to whom?" "Why, I sold them to Mr. Wallett, at the other establishment." The old lady's face flushed like a thousand roses. "Dolt! fool! idiot! you've ruined me! Pack up your traps, and leave at once." Here her rage overcame her, and she fell back into the arms of one of her attendants. However, her case was not so serious as at first imagined. A little cold gin and water recalled her to consciousness, and three pinches of snuff restored her usual equanimity. Of course, contributing so largely to the success of the concern, I was a great favourite with the manager. Attractive actors always are. But the tide of my affairs was now at high water mark. The proprietor was a man of means, and had many comforts. Although he generally lived at the best hotels, he still had, near the establishment, what is called a "living waggon;" so that at fairs, and such occasions, he and his family might be on the spot, to attend to business. As they sometimes had to travel all night, the waggon was fitted up with comfortable beds for the young people, and furnished with a stove, cooking utensils, &c. In order that the waggon might earn its own living, and thus doubly deserve its name, at the back was a set of dioramic views, vulgarly called a peep show. The lecturer on the diorama, a Scotchman named Sandy, used to describe the exhibition as "Fourteen grand pawnoramical views. Ye'll see the Hoose of Lords crooded to success, and His Majesty with a croon in his hond and a sceptre on his heed." A bystander, who had seen the show, ventured to observe that there were only eight views. Sandy coolly replied, "But the meester's aboot to get sax mair, and then there'll be fourteen." This compound structure, carrying hotel and fine art gallery on two wheels, was ordained to cause the overthrow of my prosperity. Early one morning, breakfast was being prepared in the hotel department, the cooking apparatus of which was close to the grand front entrance, approached by steps placed between the shafts. We were about making some alterations in the battlements of the Towers of Warsaw, and it was necessary that the engineers should remove the locomotive hotel and gallery. Being a self-commissioned captain of the engineer corps, I took command of the shafts, had the props which supported them removed, and while several subordinates applied their strength to the wheels, I undertook the direction of the movements. As I mentioned, breakfast was preparing; there was a glowing fire, and our hunger was excited by a delicious smell of coffee and toast, and a still more exquisite odour of ham and eggs. A female's voice was heard, "Breakfast's ready; Thorne, come in." But as there's many a slip between the cup and the lip, Thorne was prevented from entering the saloon. At that moment the stout lady within walked to the rear of the hotel, then balanced on the two wheels, throwing the extra weight of fourteen stone behind. Up went the shafts, throwing me into the air as if tossed by an elephant, the shafts acting as his tusks. The lady was cast on the bed, where she was followed like lightning by the coals from the fire, and the beautiful and savoury provisions for breakfast piled in most admired disorder, and served upon broken crockery. Descending from my upward flight, luckily for myself I did not fall on the pavement, which might have broken my neck, and thus saved my friends much trouble, and spared you the infliction of reading this book. More fortunately, I dropped through the open door of the waggon, and alighted on the singular conglomeration at the back. I crawled quickly away from the steaming coffee, burning coals, and prostrate stout lady, thinking the situation would be too hot for me. I believe the lady was rescued without having sustained much injury, and the burning coals, which left their mark on the sheets and blankets, were extinguished by a few pailsful of water. This I learned by report; for as soon as I found myself outside, I made what the Yankees call "tall walking" towards my hotel, and departed thence for parts unknown.

This untoward accident I of course much regretted, as I had received great kindness from the worthy proprietor. He had a son for whom I had a great respect. He was an only son, and like other only sons as a rule, was a spoiled child. He was allowed money to almost any unreasonable extent. As we did not receive regular salaries, but were remunerated according to business done, and had no check upon receipts and payments, we were consequently entirely at the mercy of the paymaster-general. Under these circumstances we all considered that we had an interest for the time being in all money taken, which accounts for the following occurrence. As there were several other large establishments frequenting the same fairs, we were compelled to display outside our most powerful attractions, to draw the vast crowds to our show. My old cynic experience and my slight skill as a *modelatori* were brought into requisition. I therefore designed and executed a large dragon, with tremendous jaws, claws, and wings, worked by a strong man inside, whose limbs formed the legs of the dragon. This reptile was colossal in size and hideous in appearance, and was a source of great fear and tribulation to youug Thorne, to dispel whose terror I took no particular pains. In order to get paid for my trouble in creating the monster, I nailed up a few laths in a corner under the stage to imitate a den, and told the youngster that if he did not give me all the money his mother gave him to waste, to purchase food for the dragon, the first time he felt hungry the boy must be devoured to make him a meal. With such parents and such a son you may be sure the dragon was kept in splendid condition. But when the waggon upset, and the poor dragon was left to the promiscuous charity of an unreeling world, he doubtless perished by sheer starvation.

My next engagement was with Holloway's Amphitheatre at Sheffield. This was an enormous temporary building erected by Mr. Ducrow for a circus. Mr. Ducrow had ruined his own season, and brought the building into disrepute by his hasty temper. The Master Cutler, and most of the *élite* of the neighbourhood came to patronize the performance one night. Some forty or fifty carriages were drawn up in front of the circus, headed by the Master Cutler, who sent in his card to Ducrow, whom he expected to do the honours of his establishment by welcoming his patrons. But Ducrow returned a message saying that Ducrow only waited upon the Queen of England and not upon a set of dirty knife-grinders. They were so indignant that they turned their horses' heads round, proceeded to the Town Hall, improvised a band, and spent the evening with a ball instead of the circus entertainment.

We opened with a very powerful company and a large stud of horses. But the support we received was so slight that the performing bipeds and quadrupeds frequently outnumbered the spectators. It was at this establishment that I made my first appearance on the sawdust. As a rule clowns, acrobats, gymnasts, and the like are bad riders. So it happened that on the first night, in a twelve-horse entrée, five of the twelve riders were *hors de combat*. Two of the clowns were much hurt, one having three fingers broken. This rendered it necessary to fill the places of the mutilated horse comedians. As I was engaged as clown in the pantomime, as "Simkins" in the ballets, and as posturer between the pieces, my line somewhat assimilated to the arena. I must here remark that though five horsemen out of twelve were lost in the charge, this circumstance very slightly injured the effect of the entrée. Though one of the missing horsemen was the head of a division, his old horse Sam, a spotted one who had been in the circus twenty years, nobly led his column with unerring precision, though there was only one rider left out of six, and he brought up the rear. This mounted horse however was the only one that made a mistake. In his dilemma, the manager asked me as a favour to go into two acts in the arena. Always happy to oblige, I immediately consented, and being furnished with a dress by one of the disabled clowns, made my first appearance as an equestrian clown. On my entrance I felt somewhat confused by being surrounded by the audience, but soon overcame that little difficulty, and dashed into my part with my usual energy. With a local song or two of my own composing, hits at the times, and my posturing, which I could always fall back upon, I soon became a great favourite with very small audiences. It was part of my contract with the manager that I should have a benefit during the season on the usual terms; but on account of my undertaking extra duty in the circus Mr. Holloway kindly proffered me, by way of recompense, half a clear benefit. According to the usual run of business this would have brought me in about two pounds, which would barely have paid half the printing expenses. So I determined to have recourse to what is professionally called "gagging." I advertised a new drama, "The Life and Death of Napoleon, in three acts, representing Moscow, Waterloo, and St. Helena.—To sing a local song, written by myself, mounted on another donkey.—The grand fashionable night of the season.—A splendid military spectacle—100 men and horses on the stage at once!" This we could have managed, as far as men and horses were concerned, but unfortunately we had not a soldier's jacket in the establishment, or any other military equipments or stores except what we could hire or borrow at second-hand shops. You can easily imagine the motley troops that would have been raised—a Falstaffian army, such as Sir John was ashamed to march through Coventry. A single company, according to uniforms, would be composed of marines, lancers, dragoons, buglers, drummers, infantry, with here and there the long-waisted, long-lapped, blue-cuffed coat of the original volunteers. A uniform of the class that Sir Henry Smith, of Bearchurch Hall, wore at the Colchester review, when the great and good Prince Albert rode up and said to him, "Excuse me, sir, but I'm admiring your ancient costume;" and laying his hand upon Sir Henry's sleeve, the Prince said, "They don't make such cloth as that now." When the veteran replied, "No, your Royal Highness, nor such men either." It was a severe winter; the snow was knee deep, and on my benefit day the sun was bright. I persuaded the manager to allow the band and carriage to go round the town to wake up the natives. I had made up my mind as to my plan of operations. I kept my horse back in his stall till the procession had got some distance from the theatre, when I knew they durst not return, and then prepared to follow them. I was lodging at the time with an old coachman of the name of Midgely, from whom I had borrowed an old driving coat, something like that which brought our friend Jones to grief. Dressed in this coat, with a woman's night cap on my head, surmounted by an old hat, with a handkerchief over that, tied under my chin à la Molly Mollony, and with a sheet of mill-board in front of me on which was written "Wallett's Benefit Night —100 men and horses." I then sallied forth, and soon overtook the cavalcade, to their disgust and sorrow, for my appearance was the signal for a volley of a thousand snow-balls, more or less. With my stout double-milled kersey coat, my mill-board cuirass, and my head improperly protected as it was, the snowy missiles fell harmlessly on my armour, and my security afforded me a fine opportunity of enjoying the discomfiture of the rest of the procession. Of course I took every opportunity of bringing them successively into the thickest of the fire, by at one time riding up to the band carriage and desiring the driver to pull up at a public house to treat the musicians. The halt of the carriage was saluted till the vehicle was filled with snow-balls, the musicians' hats knocked off, and their instruments damaged. I then fell back to shake hands with some of the equestrians, and give them a cheering word, when my presence alongside attracted a shower of balls from thousands of boys who lined the streets and surrounded us. The public at which we pulled up was called the Pump Tavern, which greatly mystified Mr. Holloway, for the carpenters, grooms, &c., using this house, the name of which was unknown to him, when he accused any of them of being drunk was assured "I have not had anything stronger than what came from the pump to-day." In due time we returned to the theatre, and with the exception of two or three riders who ascertained their exact length by measuring it in the snow, and the right energetic cannonading with polar ammunition, all passed off pleasantly. But over their dinners I believe they breathed a prayer for me, "a prayer I did not hear," but can guess its tenour and fervency.

Night came, by far the greatest success of the season. We took £33. Everything went wrong; half the supers never came near. The piece altogether was a concoction from three dramas of which we had no books. Two-thirds of the company had never seen the pieces, and myself and the others had only a very imperfect acquaintance with the matter, either histrionic or historical. The actors evidently anticipated a row, if not the pulling down of the theatre, and one by one came to me, saying, "You'll not require me any more in this piece?" To which I replied, "All right, my boy, all right." At length I found I had but one adherent, the leading man, Mr. John Shean, who stuck to me, even in my exile at St. Helena, and saw the last of his illustrious master. The different battles were done outside the stage to order, by drums, trumpets, gongs, and occasionally a battery of maroons. We certainly should have had the burning of Moscow, only some fellow accidentally threw a quart of ale on the red fire, which entirely extinquished the burning of the city. This was my first appearance as Napoleon. My costume was accurate in style, but rather inferior as to material. It consisted of a blue livery coat, faced with white calico, a pair of Wellington boots with paste board extensions, *à la* Napoleon. A billycock hat, turned up in the proper form, with a pair of threepenny Berlin gloves, and white drawers, completed the picture of the great Emperor. At length the play concluded, and the war ended on the stage, but a hurricane commenced in the front. Instead of snowballing, we had a shower of ginger beer bottles. They demanded my appearance. I came forward, and was greeted with yells and execrations that none but a Dante could describe. "There is no tide in the wildest passion but has an ebb;" and peace having been gradually restored, I addressed the audience thus—"Ladies and gentlemen, we have been here for upwards of three months. The manager has lost above £100 a week. There has never been anything advertised on the bills that has not been faithfully performed on the stage. He never promised anything but what he could do, and you never came.

D

I advertised what I knew we never should or could do, and you have come; and I am very much obliged to you."

The next part of the performance was in the arena, which went off most vociferously. As I had then been schooled to play clown to very thin houses, you may be sure that a full house gave me an extra impetus, and I went in with such a hearty good will and *abandon* that soon dissipated the clouds of displeasure. "All's well that ends well." But the end was not yet. For my next appearance was, as I before stated, to sing, mounted upon an ass, a local song written by myself. It was a milkman's ass, and was his first appearance upon any stage. He must have been labouring under what is called a stage fright, for on the ascending of the curtain, in spite of force or entreaties, he resolutely refused to face the music. The symphony played, but no donkey or singer appeared. Dissatisfaction was rapidly developing itself. But it had no impression upon him; go he would not. There was but one course left: to drop the curtain, bring the ass on to the centre of the stage, mount him, and then again raise the curtain—what is called in theatrical parlance, "a discovery." But "the best laid schemes of mice and men aft gang agee." So it turned out. The poor donkey, with distended nostrils and extended ears, gave one astonished stare at the scene before him, and with a loud hee-haw galloped off the stage, and behind the scenes, carrying with him his poetical rider—who did not expect his Pegasus to prove so lively—and the undelivered comic song. However, my motto through life has been "Nil desperandum." The curtain again dropped, and being raised, I was rediscovered on the donkey. With a salver of oats before him, he permitted me to warble forth my local ditty, while he amused himself with a mouthful of corn, which he masticated with apparent gusto, and seemed rather to enjoy his novel situation. Thus ended my first benefit at Sheffield.

At that time I used a house opposite the theatre, called "The Traveller's Rest," kept by William Hunter, where I adjourned for refreshment after the labours of the evening. The private bar, or counter, was screened by a crimson curtain, through which you could hear all that was passing at the public counter. Mrs. Hunter was in the secret, and inquired of the customers as they came in, "Have you been to the theatre to-night?" The reply was generally given in language unfit for ears polite. She then inquired, "What do you think of Mr. Wallett?" Of course there were various opinions, but from what I overheard, the majority had arrived at this conviction, that Mr. Wallett was a very clever fellow, but a great liar. "One hundred men and horses," said one, "and the battle of Waterloo! Why we never saw more than ten men, and not a horse at all till the circus began!" However, in time they kindly forgave my deception, but never forgot it. Twenty-five years after this, I had another benefit at the magnificent stone amphitheatre built by Mr. James Ryan. Late in the afternoon of my benefit day, a gentleman, one of the principal physicians of the town, drove up to the hotel. He was shown into my apartments, when he stated he had made up a large party at his house, to patronize me that evening, and had called at the box office to secure places, but was too late, the office being closed. He therefore called upon me, in order to obtain tickets for the boxes. I thanked him kindly, and told him, what I repeat now, that I never had a ticket printed to my name, that I never sold one, even to a friend, or under any pretence. For I have always believed, and am still of opinion, that hawking tickets from publichouse to publichouse, from grocer to baker—or worse, eternally boring your friends—has done more to lessen theatrical and circus people in the eyes of the public than all the peccadilloes and faults they have ever committed. Oh, reform it altogether! I promised to see the box-keeper, and secure seats for his party. He warmly congratulated me upon the success I had met with in life, took a friendly farewell, and left me; but the door was scarcely closed before a little knock was heard. The door opened again, the good honest face of the Yorkshire doctor intruded. With a radiant smile and an arch twinkle of his eyes, he said, "It's not one hundred men and horses this time, eh, Wallett? Good day."

The season ended as unfortunately as it began. When I say unfortunately, I mean for the manager, for the actors suffered nothing, being paid to the uttermost farthing. They sympathized however with Mr. Holloway, who notwithstanding ruinous business paid them punctually every Saturday. John Shean, the leading actor, going into the treasury for his salary towards the end of his long and costly campaign, said in the fulness of his heart, "I should be content, and so would several others, to take half our salaries for the remainder of the season; really the business has been something fearful, and from my heart I pity you." The manager, a high-couraged gentleman, who saw no credit in merely doing what was right, replied, "If I had taken £1000 a week I should not have given you one shilling more, Mr. Shean. Don't you pity me, sir. Take your money, sir. Hang your pity, sir." I was the next on the salary list and found our friend in a towering passion. As I entered he yelled out, "Now, young gentleman, here's your money, take it, and hook it. Hang your pity. Jack Shean's been pitying me. I don't want any of your pity. Send in the other fellows." As the door closed I heard him still emphatically repudiating our pity.

At the close of the season the company was divided; the theatrical portion went to Liverpool, and the equestrians formed a separate troupe. A circus had been erected opposite the Woodman Inn, at Wakefield, kept by our old friend Briggs. It was the first equestrian company that had been in Wakefield for upwards of twenty years. The success was enormous. It was here that I first assumed the title of "The Shakesperian Jester."

My predecessor, in the last company that visited the town, was little Webber, who was killed next door to where our circus stood, by falling down the area of the partially erected news-rooms. Though I never saw him, I still had the respect for a brother-actor to repair his gravestone, which had become dilapidated, and plant a weeping willow over it in the churchyard of St. John's. Our establishment went by the name of Wells and Miller's. Here I was taken by the hand and fostered; and if there be aught about me worthy of admiration, the world may thank the kindly influences of the people of Wakefield for its development. We here made so much money that we all became saucy and disagreeable. Everybody quarrelled with everybody. The partnership of Wells and Miller was dissolved, and the stock divided after a novel manner. Each partner selected one article in turn, until the whole of the stud and property divided, except a 12-ft. ladder which remained. Mr. John Wells proposed to toss up for it, but Miller would have it divided between them. Whereupon Wells wanted to saw it across, thus making two useful 6-ft. ladders; but no! the other mountebank, acting the dog in the manger, or equestrian Shylock, would have his pound of flesh. He insisted upon having half a 12-ft. ladder, and would have it sawn down the centre of the rounds, thus rendering both portions useless. This brought to a conclusion a season whose only drawback was its prosperity.

The separated partners starting each on his own account, I remained with John Wells, who erected a very fine circus at Dewsbury. There were two gentlemen known by the name of Jack Wells. One was our manager and the other a celebrated clown at Cooke's. They were distinguished as "little" and "big Jack Wells." The season at Dewsbury was the worst I have ever known either before or since. It was there that Billy Seal, the clown, made his first appearance. The affair ended with a serious loss to the manager, who discovered to his cost that there are shoddy men with shoddy souls, as inferior as the material they manufacture.

I next joined Samwells's "Royal Circus, patronized by William IV. and Queen Adelaide," as stated in large letters outside the show. The principal entrance to this Royal Circus was through a large slit in a tarpaulin. It was at Bradford Fair, and the circus was erected in a wood-yard belonging to Jonas Beanland. For want of better accommodation we all dressed in a saw-pit. During one of the evening entertainments a tremendous storm came on, and the rain poured in torrents for nearly an hour. So at the conclusion of our performance we found to our surprise and annoyance, that boxes, boots, shoes, in fact our whole wardrobes were afloat, there being some feet of water in the pit.

I remained with this company during the Christmas holidays. Charley Marsh, Tom Barry, and myself lodged together, having three beds in one large room. At that time I was very steady and regular in my habits, and after my arduous labours of posturing, clowning, &c., I was always ready for bed at a reasonable hour. However I had no sooner began to doze before Marsh would come in and awaken me to tell me of some jolly lark or curious incident. We would talk ourselves to sleep, when our friend Barry would arrive, and arouse us to hear the story of his adventures. Then followed a grand melée of pillows, bolsters, boots and shoes flying through the air the moment the candle was extinguished. This you would imagine to be the last of the night's performance. But not so. Just as downy sleep lightly pressed our eyelids, a band of music would announce the approach of Christmas. Night after night I bore this sore infliction, until the time arrived when endurance ceased to be a virtue, for I received additional provocation. The waits arrived with a reinforcement of singers. I could bear it no longer, but springing out of bed, I collected all the slops I could find, determined to give them a bumper at parting. Tying my handkerchief over my head, I looked out of the window, and asked them in a feigned voice, "How many are there of you?" The reply was, "There's twelve on us, sir." I then bawled out, "Then share that among you." All was dark as the grave; there was a sudden dash and splash, and then silence. At length poor Billy Marsden, who played the violoncello, exclaimed in a most sorrowful tone to his companions, " Ah, lads, he's spoilt bass!"

Not being happy in my surroundings with the Royal Circus Company, I again returned to my friend Thorne, of the Towers of Warsaw notoriety, by whom I was gladly received and installed as acting manager. Mr. Thorne was generally speaking, a steady man, and attentive to business, but would occasionally indulge in a spree for a week or two together. He happened to be on one of these freaks soon after I joined him at Barnsley, his wife being confined at the time in Sheffield. He started to visit her the day before our opening. Though he spent more than a week on the road he never reached Sheffield or returned to Barnsley. He used to sit and drink at a way-side house, and when he heard the horn announce the approach of a Sheffield coach, rushed outside, and mounted on the roof. But his unquenchable thirst always compelled him to alight at the first public house, where of course he was left behind. There he would enjoy himself, till a coach going the other way picked him up and returned him to his former quarters. Thus vibrating between house and house by every passing coach, he spent his days and nights. He had left no one to look after his interests except his daughter Bella, ten or twelve years of age. So of course the entire duty of money taker, check taker, secretary, and general comptroller devolved on me. I before explained that regular salaries were not paid at this establishment, but merely shares of the takings. Our business was immense. Crowded nightly from pit to dome, to use a theatrical phrase. The proprietor being away, I and the company having had all the work to do, and knowing he had made plenty of money out of us before, and thought but little of us or our services, we thought as little of him, and had a jolly time of it. You may judge. For on the arrival of Mr. Thorne in the town, after near a fortnight's absence, with a weary body and foggy mind, he ran against a well-dressed gentleman in the street, and inquired the way to the Towers of Warsaw. This gentleman was no other than John Hughes, a relative, and a caterer for the refreshment saloon; but so altered in appearance that I suppose Thorne took him for a clergyman. John soon revealed himself. "Governor, why, don't you know me? I'm Jack Hughes. Eh, governor, we've been doing a roaring business!" To which the manager replied, "Yes, you look as if you had." Hearing the prosperous state of affairs, the good news partially aroused him from his lethargy, and made him for a moment forget the money he had spent, and the valuable time he had wasted. He hastened to his home (before described—the heterogeneous peripatetic dioramic hotel, which I upset) where his daughter gave a glowing description of the world of wealth we had acquired. "Well," said he, "where's the money?" "I never had it," said she. "No, who had?" "Why, Mr. Wallett." I was sent for. "You've been doing great business, I hear." "Oh, first rate, governor," said I. "And what have you done with the money?" "What should I do with it? As this is a sharing company, I shared it among the people nightly; and you will be delighted to see how happy they are, and how well dressed. They will be a credit to you and your establishment. They one and all behaved so well that I shared every shilling among them, and took no extra portion for my management. But as a mark of our disapprobation of your conduct in leaving us at the mercy of the waves, to sink or swim, we have left you the ground rent, the gas, and the printing to pay." I of course expected to be what the drapers would call " swapped," but was not.

Our next stand was at Bingley, where a very pleasant circumstance occurred. We were erecting the large booth, when the vicar came up, and addressing me, inquired, "What are you doing here?" "I am erecting a large portable theatre, sir." "Oh, indeed! have you any ladies with you?" "Oh yes, sir, we have at least twenty." "Dear me," said he, "I hope you don't represent anything immoral." I assured him we did not. I did not know at the moment who he was; but as he bade me good morning, he shook me kindly by the hand, and said, "I shall come and see you, and, in return, you must come and see me on Sunday; I'm the vicar." I promised to do so, and we both kept our words. The worthy vicar was a frequent attendant at our theatre, and, I think, never had cause to regret the countenance he gave us. We made up a large party, and on the first Sunday visited the old parish church. The subject of the sermon was the value of a good name. Valuable on earth, he said, even supposing, as infidels would make out, that there was no world to come. I must tell you that our party had been ushered into the large, scarlet-cushioned pew belonging to the minister's family, where, of course, we were the "observed of all observers," and immediately under the preacher's eye. In the course of his sermon, he quoted the entire passage from Shakespere, commencing, "A good name is the immediate jewel of my soul," delivering it with admirable emphasis. At its conclusion, he looked down upon us with a peculiar expression of face, as if to say, "I, too, am a disciple of Shakespere, and there's a sop for you in your own element." After the service, we waited for the reverend gentleman, to thank him for his kind invitation, and the accommodation afforded, and also for the high intellectual treat we had enjoyed. This was one of the pleasantest episodes of my life.

So far so good; but there has always been a squeeze of lemon in my pleasantest draught. My luck again! You remember the boy who fed the dragon. He had become my pupil again, and I taught him some of the devildom that often possessed me in my youth. The Towers of Warsaw were erected on a small piece of ground near the main thoroughfare, through which most of the congregation passed on their way home from church. My friend and companion at the time was John Smallwood, commonly known as "Honest John." We were walking arm-in-arm in the long stream of returning worshippers, when, just as we passed the door of the theatre, to the amusement of the vast concourse, and to my great horror, the boy Dick Thorne slipped out unseen by us, with a large red-hot poker used in the pantomime. He inserted this weapon between my coat tails and the nether portion of my person. Turning round, and discovering the cause of the hearty peal of laughter that burst from the crowd, there was nothing left for me but a hasty flight. But Dick, who had become a big boy, could run nearly as fast as I, and, poker in hand, he kept up the hot chase till we arrived at home. Where, for the trouble the youth had taken, and the annoyance he had given me, he received a lesson in a noble accomplishment, called in pantomimic lingo, " Napping the slap."

Soon after this, I transferred my services from Thorne's to the opposition establishment, Old Wild's, where I formed an intimacy with one of the sons, Sam, that has lasted through life. In fact, I may say, as Burns, " I lo'ed him like a very brither." As we had a very happy and prosperous time, Sam and I had saved a few pounds. We determined upon a trip to my native town, to see my parents, brothers and sisters, a goodly array, as I am the eldest of twenty-four children. Being young fellows, and fond of life, our funds were soon exhausted. We did not like to write to his mother for money, as we had run away and were neglecting our business, and my mother had none to give us. But there's always balm in Gilead. It was within three days of Hull fair; and, to our unspeakable joy, old Jones arrived with his booth. We were immediately engaged as stars in this small firmament, at the princely salary of one guinea each per day. It was on the evening after we made this engagement, when Sam and I were seated in the bar of Glover's Hotel, that an elderly gentleman, with either a very high forehead or a partially bald head, attracted our attention by his steadfast gaze upon me. At length, some one mentioning my name, the stranger of the lofty brow rushed across the room, and clasping me by both hands, exclaimed, " I thought 'twas you, my dear boy; you've dropped from the clouds." He then made himself known to us as Mr. Gifford, the stage manager of the Old Theatre Royal, Hull. It appeared that they were producing a pantomime for the Hull fair, and had engaged artists from London, Signor Garcia and young Masoura, as clown and pantaloon. The pantomime was to be produced on the following night. The steamboats from London were all in, and there was no railway at that time. The management had given up all hope of the party arriving by mail coach; the journey being long and expensive. This then was my first essay in management, for I forthwith made a contract to supply the pantomimic characters for £8 a night. I played the clown, and Sam Wild the pantaloon. A very clever fellow of the name of Plimerina, who had married one of the dancers of the theatre, a native of Hull, happened to be here on a visit to his mother-in-law. Fortunately, I had met them that day, and ascertained they had nothing to do, so I secured their services as harlequin and columbine. So it was the first opportunity I had of obeying the injunction, "Put money in thy purse." We instantly waited upon old Jones, who contrary to the opinion of the outside world, though a showman had a Christian heart within him, and told him the nature of our engagements. We said we would work at his establishment from noon till nine at night, when we must leave to appear in the pantomime. He said, "Bless you, my boys, I have children of my own. Don't let me be any bar to your preferment, I like my children to get on in the world. There's our Sally, that's Tom's wife; see how I've brought her on! she'd make one of the best actresses in the world if she could only read. But we get over that difficulty. I read the parts to her, and she gets them off." So, as Wallett and Wild at the show, and as Signor Garcia and young Masoura at the Theatre Royal, assisted by Plimerina and his wife; receiving two guineas from the show, and eight pounds from the theatre, and paying one pound a night to harlequin and columbine, and two pounds to my chum and brother Sam for his day and night, I was left with a handsome margin of profit. All went on merrily as marriage bells for some time. But my luck again! Old mother Wild arrived with a policeman from Hull, to snatch us from our prosperity, and drag us back to that theatrical factory where labour was certain and payment rather doubtful. With much ado we persuaded the old lady to allow us to remain till the end of the week, undertaking to return on the following Monday, which we accordingly did. We had only been absent two short weeks, but discovered the truth of the old adage, "When the cat's away the mice will play." I found the place in chaotic confusion. There was nought but neglect and insubordination, and on my arrival I found that the whole of the *troupe mauvais* had openly rebelled and mutinied. They were passing their time in the very unprofitable manner of singing,

> "Under the shady greenwood tree,
> We merry merry archers roam."

In a public-house kept by a man of the name of Borrill, this refrain was parodied by our old friend Jemmy Wild, thus:—

> "Under the shady greenwood tree,
> Very good swill, Mr. Borrill."

We soon prepared to move on from our position at Marsh Lane *vulgè* Martch Loin. While I was busy screwing a cap on a waggon wheel I was wantonly attacked by six stalwart men, led on by an Irish actor, called Paddy Hall, six feet high. He cowardly struck me, then only a stripling, when not a friend was near me. I stood up and said, "Hall, if you repeat that be prepared for the consequences." He grinned a laugh, and again struck me. I held in my hand the heavy screw wrench I had been using, and striking him on the top of the head, felled him like a dog. He rose again, and rushed at me, and seized me by the throat; but a fountain of blood that played on the top of his head and descended on all sides soon made him relax his powerful grasp, and looking at me with glazed eyes, he fell back upon the ground. He was carried away by his sympathizing friends, not one of whom had the courage to face the stripling, and resent the injury done to their leader. The effect of the blow of the moment lasted a considerable time, during which he was in the infirmary: while I supported his wife and only child, as some atonement for having descended to the level of a blackguard. It again appeared as if I were fated to be the cause of this man's death. Months after, when we were on terms of the greatest amity, I happened to take up a pistol on the stage one night, when it exploded at half-cock, and blew away one of his cheeks, part of his tongue, and some of his teeth. So much did this second injury prey upon my mind, that I determined never to take another engagement with Paddy Hall.

There was a manager named John Collins, who married Margaret, a daughter of old Mr. Parish, and was once the lessee of the Adelphi Theatre, at Hull. At the end of his Hull season, I joined him in a theatrical booth for a provincial tour through several lively and thriving cities, such as Cottingham, Beverley, Driffield, Market Weighton, &c. After many vicissitudes, our corps dramatique left us one by one, till none but the manager, his brother William, a musician, and myself were left. Then came our difficulty. But we happened to have a palace scene, an interior, with a long perspective, which left the centre arch not more than three feet in altitude. I observed this, and said to the manager, "This shall be our salvation." I cut out the centre view of that arch, and thereby formed an elegant little proscenium for a theatre fantoccini. With the aid of Mrs. Collins, Clisby Webster, William Collins, myself, and a good sharp knife, there was created in less than a week an entire dramatic and acrobatic troupe. For I having had some practice in this line before, while I was with the establishment of Mons. Maffet, knew all the ins and outs and intricacies of the dancing dollies. Again, when Mumford and Calver had the theatre of Lilliput in the Apollo Saloon at Hull, and they made so much money that they had to wheel the coppers away every morning in a barrow. Mumford threw poor Calver overboard with a wife and several children. Then, though only a mere lad, I rushed to the rescue, and with the assistance of Mary Ann Short and her sisters, made poor Calver one of the finest sets of figures that ever simulated life. On the night when Mumford and Calver were to part, the former was invited after the performance to sup with the Short family; and after supper, by way of a *bonne bouche*, the figures were one by one, in splendid array, and the very perfection of mechanism, introduced to his astonished gaze. Knowing that he did well, and that his son after him made a fortune by an establishment in which some of my blockheads were principal performers, I resolved that, as we had no flesh and blood actors left, we would have wooden ones. So I manufactured the usual gymnasts, the common clown, the everlasting pantaloon, the dancing skeleton, and above all the great and irresistible attraction—the Babes in the Wood, the cruel uncle, and the blessed birds, their undertakers. We had no more disaffection in the company, no more round-robins, no more strikes for arrears of salaries, no more growling because everybody could not play Richard III., no more drunken comic singers who having forgotten their songs looked down upon the leader in the orchestra, endeavouring to lay the blame on him. Performances were judiciously carried through, and the actors and actresses safely locked up in a box at the close in perfect peace and harmony. Thus we managed to live, which before we found impossible. But my luck again! Wandering through the town I saw a ham hanging at a shop door. It was a fine one, and a ticket announced it might be purchased for fourpence halfpenny a pound. Having ever an eye for a bargain, I stepped in and inquired how it was that so fine a ham was to be had for so low a price. The shopman informed me that it had been a very bad season for curing hams; and though the ham was really good for immediate use it would not keep long enough to realise the usual market price. So I bought it; but, alas, the cooking of it! Our booth was built near the centre of the market place at Selby, the whole square of which was macadamised, but was crossed at various angles by narrow flag paving. One of these courses ran through our Theatre du Petite Lazarre. There had been a great deal of wet weather, and the porous stones had absorbed a large quantity of water, and held some in cavities. Having borrowed a large kettle, with three stakes we made a tripod *à la* Bohemia. The fire was kindled upon one of the flagstones in the crossing. It was Sunday morning. All went on pleasantly for a time; the blazing fire made the pot bubble, and the savoury smell regaled our eager nostrils. The descending heat, however, had a less genial influence. The sudden generation of steam or gas in the stone beneath caused an explosion. A tremendous crash! up went the pot and ham through the canvas roof, down went the expectant diners on their backs.

I was for a long time happily associated with one of the most respectable firms that ever catered for the public amusement, poor dear old Rennie Colombia, properly Colombier, and his kind, motherly wife! They were universally respected wherever they went. I joined them at Ormskirk in Lancashire. There was a gentleman of the town, a great admirer of theatricals, and a liberal patron. His name was Harriott. If any of his family should read this, let me bear to them my humble testimony to his liberality. When benefits were on, he used to take a certain number of tickets from each beneficiary. On my benefit night, however, my friend was out of town. On his return, a few days after, we met in the smoke room of the hotel opposite the theatre. The room was very full. He took the opportunity to slip into my hand a neatly folded letter. I opened it, and read as follows:—

"MY DEAR MR. WALLETT—Having much admired your talent as an actor, and appreciated your conduct as a man, I should like to show to you by something more than words, that you are appreciated by me. I much regret my absence from home on your benefit night, and had not imperative business called me away, I should certainly have been with you, accompanied by a large party. But I am happy to hear that you had a great house without our assistance. However, I must beg your acceptance of the enclosed trifle, as a recognition of your rare talent."

The "enclosed trifle," was a £5 Bank of England note. At that time I was poor and needy, had an aged father and mother to support, and several younger brothers and sisters to rear and educate, but I could not afford to become a pauper and receive a gratuity. I instantly rose, and said, "Gentlemen, I have great pleasure in acknowledging a splendid gift from our friend Mr. Harriott, this evening. As he could not attend on my benefit night, he has kindly presented me with £5." Loud applause from all parts of the room. "But, gentlemen, I have laid down a rule, from which I intend never to deviate. I have never sold a ticket in my life, and I never will. I follow my profession as a legitimate source of livelihood, and when it ceases to support me without having to accept gratuities, or hawk pasteboards, I'll leave it altogether, and for ever. Under these circumstances, Mr. Harriott, I'm sure, will excuse me when I say that I most respectfully return his noble present. May God bless the heart that prompted such goodness; and I hope the recollection of his munificence will be impressed upon my mind many years after that note has ceased to circulate." There were many of my professional brethren present, who, like most of the brethren of the great human family, are prone to suspect the motives of others. They re-christened me "Mr. Bounce," saying the gift was not enough for my honour and glory, and that I was vexed because it was not £10. But my generous friend and I parted with a proper understanding of each other, and years after that we met, not as the giver and receiver of a dole, but as equal men, honourable in our transactions, and noble in our aspirations.

I remained after this for a considerable period in various establishments on the "walk-'em-up" line. First with old Lowe. I joined him at Bilston, Staffordshire, to supply the place of Joe Wildman, who called himself "funny Joe," but who might have been more appropriately called "dirty Joe." Though I have seen thousands of better clowns, both cis-atlantic and trans-atlantic, I never saw a dirtier one than he. On my first appearance, he was engaged at an opposition show-shop, when his polished wit burst out into the following machine poetry—

"Old Lowe has discharged funny Joe,
But when the great clown away does go,
Then old Lowe will be glad again of funny Joe."

It was here I met, in his early struggling, the child that was father to the man destined to obtain a world-wide popularity. I mean John Anderson, better known as the "Wizard of the North." It was here, too, that I met James Wesley, Henry Pointer, William Potts, Charley Blacker, Susan Scott, and many others for whom I had a great respect. Nearly all have gone to "that undiscovered country from whose bourne no traveller returns." Peace be with them.

I had also a long and profitable engagement with Mr. James Romain, and nearly finished my brilliant career with him. He was very fond of fireworks, and engaged as pyrotechnist an Irishman called Absalom Thornton. One morning, at rehearsal, Absalom sat astride upon one of the pit seats, mealing gunpowder. It seems that the leather bag in which they generally powdered it was out of repair, so Absalom invented a new mode, namely rubbing it down with a flat iron on a seat board. To his left he had spread out a sheet of brown paper, to his right an open barrel of twenty pounds of powder, and a quantity mealing on the seat between his legs. He held in his mouth a short black pipe, which he was smoking away as for dear life. As he ground the powder with his flat iron to the tune of

"Oliver Cromwell did her pumwell,
    And he made a breach in her battlements,"

I discovered the fearful position in which forty or fifty persons were placed. I pointed out the danger to the manager, at the same time calling to Thornton, " Come up quick here; your wife's in a fit." He rushed on the stage, when the angry manager gave him a hit under the ear enough to make a breach in his battlements. And thus we all escaped sudden death, almost by the skin of our teeth. Shortly afterwards poor Romain came to a violent end. He was walking round his establishment one dark night, guarding his property, in one of the badger towns of Lancashire, when some ruffian threw a brick and killed him on the spot. He was an Irishman by birth, and for truth, honesty, and kindness his nation never produced a better man. Blessed be his memory.

I now bade farewell to my professional brethren in this particular line, leaving them with the conviction that however high my utmost efforts might raise me, I should never meet with more hospitable or warm-hearted friends than I left behind me in the humble Thespian booths.

CHAPTER IV.

"The play's the thing."—HAMLET.

MY next engagement was with Mr. Jackman, at the Theatre, Redditch. It was here that I had the honour of becoming acquainted with dear Harry Hartley, Fenton, and the present great tragedian, Mr. Coldock. Here also Coldock first studied the part of Master Walter in the Hunchback, under my coaching. I afterwards lost sight of him for upwards of twenty years, till I met him in Philadelphia, United States; and by a singular coincidence he was playing Master Walter the very night I called on him at the Walnut Street Theatre. I had now become a sort of hybrid animal. I had scarcely a claim on equestrian business, and as it were, had partially forfeited my claim to dramatic. I was a kind of go-between. While painting some scenes by the celebrated Batty, that had been enlarged, I received a letter from Mr. Thomas Cooke, who with his company had just arrived from America. I was engaged to open with him in Hull as a regular circus clown. I also agreed to paint, model, and make all properties required for the equestrian pieces, including chandeliers, dragons, &c.; so you may be sure I had but little leisure time on hand, especially as all their properties had been destroyed by fire in America. There was only a week previous to the production of each piece to produce every thing required for it. However, to youth and energy nearly all things are possible, and all were ready. My success in the ring was unequivocal. I at once jumped into public favour.

I had here a fine opportunity for fighting a duel had it been in my line. There was a swell dentist called Mann in the town, who lived in great style, dined with and gave dinners to officers, in fact he was a great card. A brother clown of mine, called Dewhurst, during a feigned quarrel in the ring, told me that if I did not retract what I said he would knock my teeth out. The illustrious dentist and several officers from the barracks were in the boxes. So I replied to Dewhurst, "You may be the man that can knock my teeth out, but you are not the Mann that can put them in again." He challenged me, but I got over that trouble in my usual way. I did not refuse to meet him, but stipulated that instead of pistols there should be but one weapon, a horsewhip, and that I should use it. I began to fancy myself of some consequence in the world, for within a month I received another challenge. It happened thus: I, John Proudley, William Mears, and Jemmy Allison, were to attend a ball held in the fashionable region of Salt House Lane. A young man named Glover had started a hairdressing saloon in front of the Old Summer Theatre. I called there on my way to the ball, to have my hair dressed *à la mode*. The perfumer was an old friend, and gave me half-a-dozen of his cards to place in the dressing rooms of the circus by way of advertisement. I promised to further his interest in this way, and carefully packed his cards in my vest pocket. The early part of the ball passed off very agreeably. But about one in the morning, came in two or three young officers, who had been dining out, and were half full of wine, and the balance filled up with mischief. They were not long before they made themselves as disagreeable as they could have desired to be. At length one of the fellows rudely tumbled up against my partner, when I, in as gentle a manner as circumstances would permit, endeavoured to explain the necessity of better conduct, out of respect to the lady, and out of consideration for his own bones; which gave him and his companions an opportunity of obtaining what they probably came for. A general row ensued, and in the end the military were defeated by the millinery. When the battle began to hang fire, and talking took the place of fighting, one of the officers handed me his card, and demanded mine in return. Though I never had a card printed to my name I, of course pretended to feel for my card-case, and rummaging my pocket found Glover's cards, one of which I gave the intending belligerent. He, after regulating his glass to one of his variegated eyes, tore it up and threw the pieces away in disdain, saying " Come, fellows, let's go home, he's only a cursed barber." I believe a deputation waited upon Glover next day to demand an apology for an offence of which he was ignorant. So my second duel ended before it began.

Our circus was erected on Dock Green, and we were compelled to cross over an iron bridge in passing from the town to it. There were four old men, two at each end of the bridge, which opened in halves. They had been turning the bridge upwards of thirty years, until they did it mechanically and without thought. They seemed to hear nought, see nought, care for nought beside, as if they lived for one object alone, their *summum bonum* being to turn the bridge. Now it happened on my benefit night, just as the doors were about to be opened, it was near high water, and the locks and bridges were open for vessels to pass. The gates were kept open so long that several hundred persons going to the circus were impeded on the journey. Of course I felt annoyed and impatient as vessel after vessel passed and our patrons were prevented passing. A large ship, with a magnificent figure-head of Flora, was about the last. Then my stock of patience, never large, was fairly used up. I had a sheet of music in my hand, and applying the end to my mouth and using it as a speaking trumpet, I gave an excellent imitation of the dock-master's word of command, singing out, "Turn that bridge." The four automata proceeded with a portion of their life-long duty, and the bridge did turn, encountering the prow of the ship with such force as to knock Flora from her perch, to join the flowers of the ocean beneath. The loud crash, the swearing of the captain, and the laughter of the by-standers, who by this time numbered over two thousand, attracted the attention of the dock-master, who was at some distance. He roared with a voice of thunder, "Turn back that bridge," and they did so. The happy turners were all the while unconscious of any mistake, mishap or accident. At length the proper authority commanded the bridge to close. The vast concourse of people rushed across, and in a few minutes the circus was crammed in every part. On this occasion a commercial traveller, with more brandy and water than brains, had seated himself between two women of unquestionable notoriety. At that time the public by-word was "variety," with which expression, without variety, our friend the bagman kept annoying the clowns in the early part of the evening. In vain was the cry of "Turn him out" raised. He persisted in his interruption, and the house being crowded it was impossible for the police to get near him. So he felt himself master of the situation. At last my turn came, and after a hearty reception, my next salutation was "variety." I instantly stopped the performance, and said, "Ladies and gentlemen, permit me to explain. You've heard that fellow for upwards of a hundred times to-night bawling out 'variety.' You do not understand what he means. I am well acquainted with him. He lives in London. He has left a wife and children at home, without the common necessaries of life, and he comes here to-night with two of the commonest women of the town; and that's what he calls 'variety.'" He was heard no more.

After a long and prosperous season we left Hull for Gainsborough Mart; and while on our journey a pleasant interruption occurred. Some years before I was travelling through the same district in great poverty, while the winter was very severe. Towards evening, passing through a small village, I saw the bright glare of a cheerful fire issuing through a window on the snow. I looked in on a happy group assembled round the fire, and contrasted their comfortable position with my forlorn and destitute state. My worldly wealth consisted of sixpence only, and I had travelled through the snow all day without tasting food. I felt for my solitary coin, and clutched it convulsively in my hand. I remembered a long journey was still before me; but I could resist no longer. So I entered the comfortable hostelry and ordered refreshment—twopennyworth of bread and cheese and a glass of ale. The country bumpkins seated round the fire had no thought or care for me; no chair was offered, or room made for the cold and weary stranger. So much for the vaunted English hospitality. Seated under a window, far from the fire, I took my frugal meal. When I had finished I waited some time, but no change out of my sixpence was brought. I inquired of a little girl, who replied, "Grandmother has gone up stairs for change." After a time the old lady brought me nine shillings and eight pence half-penny, as if I had given her half-a-sovereign. We counted out the money. There I sat for half an hour before I could make up my mind either to take it or explain the mistake. But the temptation was too strong, and "my poverty and not my will" consented. I shall never forget the suffering I endured. I left the house feeling like a thief, as I was, and walking with all speed soon left the quiet village far in the rear. Looking round at every sound behind me, dreading that every horse or trap that overtook me was in pursuit. "The thief doth fear each bush an officer." I did not know the name of the village, the sign of the house, or the name of the people. This happened years ago. Yet here I was again at the same place and house. I immediately recognized it, and found the same little table under the window where I sat forlorn. I related the affair to Cooke's party, and confessing my crime to the old lady, of course wanted to make restitution by repaying the money. She had no recollection of the circumstances, and had never missed the money; so for a length of time she refused to take it. In the end she only consented on condition that she should treat the company with two five-shilling bowls of punch. Mr. Cooke had intended to travel a few miles further, we had only stopped to feed the horses; but he was so pleased with the kindness of the old lady, that finding she had good stabling and that there was more in the village, determined to remain all night. The news having spread, most of the best people in the village arrived and begged permission to join our party. So we had a real jolly night of it.

We made an early start next morning for Gainsborough, where we remained the Mart week, and then proceeded to Nottingham. There was a townsman, a friend of Mr. Cooke, and a constant visitor to the circus, called old Jack Hattersley. He had the bad habit of tale-bearing, and made great mischief between the Cookes and the members of their company. He suffered terribly from asthma, and was in the habit of taking a seat nightly in the orchestra just over one of the entrances to the ring of the circus. Now I determined to punish him for his mischief-making. Accordingly, on the first night of the representation of St. George and the Dragon I contrived to reverse the ordinary sides of action in the drama, so as to let off blue and red fire immediately beneath our asthmatic friend. I watched the effect of my treatment, and soon perceived symptoms resembling the gasping of gold fish in their transparent globes. The addition of a few ounces of blue fire composition then operated so violently that he was obliged to be carried over the front of the boxes into the open air, more dead than alive. It had a beneficial and lasting effect; for at any time on his intrusion the slightest hint that blue fire was to be used in the piece would hurry him off with all the alacrity that short legs and short breath would permit.

After serving Mr. Cooke in the circus and in the property room for several years, upon a very low salary paid by the manager, supplemented by very good benefits paid by the public, I received a present from him of less amount than I have frequently given to charities in a single year. This, however, was quite on a par with the treatment I constantly received from him, and the other members of the family. They rejoiced in the name of Cooke's Circus, but they were such cooks as sailors know, and so many as to spoil the broth. They never employed real equestrians or vaulters, in fact, no artists except clowns, and those they would not have engaged had any of the family possessed brains enough to don the motley. The real genius of the circus arena was the renowned Ducrow. He was the Shakspere of the sawdust stage. All the riders of the present day have been living upon their inferior imitations of his great and glorious conceptions. Cookes' claim to be considered the fathers of the profession may be in every sense disallowed. The real benefactor of equestrians, in a pecuniary point of view, was James Ryan, the builder and proprietor of the Amphitheatre, Birmingham, the Amphitheatre, Sheffield, and the great Circus, Bristol. It was he that first had the heart and honesty to give a proper remuneration for talent.

Annoyed at the ungrateful conduct I experienced, I resolved to transfer my labours to a more agreeable vineyard. The opportunity soon offered. At the commencement of the amphitheatre season at Manchester, I received an insult from one of Cooke's daughters which I could not brook, nor of course retaliate upon a lady. So I withdrew at a moment's warning, demanding an apology from her father or one of her brothers before four in the afternoon, or I should never appear with them again. On walking up the street after this event I met an American, Mr. Derious, who said to me, " I understand you have left Cooke's; if so, I can engage you." He was manager to Van Amburgh & Co., then erecting a large circus in Fountain Street, Manchester, in opposition to Cooke. After acquainting him with the facts, I invited him to dine with me at the hour the apology was due. He came, brought two friends with him as witnesses, and two stamped agreements ready drawn up. We enjoyed our dinner and a glass of good wine. It was then half-past four; no apology had arrived, so the contracts were signed; and I made the happy escape from an engagement of slavery for a pittance of five pounds a week, to comparative independence at twenty pounds a week, with a carriage and horse kept for me, and not less than four benefits a year. The ink was scarcely dry before Mr. Thomas Cooke presented himself, prepared to make an amicable arrangement. Too late! I was then in the very zenith of my popularity at Manchester, and the transference of my services to Van Amburgh's company, with the superiority of our building and entertainment, brought Cookes to grief, and they ended in bankruptcy.

The following spring I started with Van Amburgh's company, on a provincial tour with tents, and for two years I experienced the most kindly treatment and a success surpassing my most ambitious dreams. In the company we had a man named Ben Brown, an American, whose mother was an Englishwoman. When a boy he had often heard her speak of the excellency of rook pie. So when he came to England his principal desire was to taste this delicacy, anticipating an extraordinary treat. In due season we obtained some fine rooks, and gave them to the cook of the hotel, to make Ben his long-desired pie. While it was in the oven I went into the kitchen, made love to the cook, and sent her for a glass of gin, generally appreciated by these artists. Directly her back was turned I opened the oven door, carefully raised the crust of the pie, and inserted about an ounce of Cavendish tobacco. I acquainted my comrades, to put them on their guard at dinner time. The dish was placed in front of old Ben Brown, who kindly invited us to partake. We all refused, "O no, Ben," you've anticipated that pie so long, you shall have it all to yourself; we'll not rob you of a morsel." Ben cut into the pie and filled his plate with the brown gravy, so richly coloured with Cavendish. He could not manage it; but after picking a piece of the outside crust, and carefully turning it over, had ultimately to give it up. Whereupon I said, "Why, Ben, you don't appear to like your pie?" He replied, "The fact is, I can eat it, but I don't seem to hanker after it." This practical joke kept him from the enjoyment he had desired for at least thirty years.

We had also in our company an old gentleman named old Jack Clarke, a veteran of eighty years, who had been an equestrian his entire life. His daughter was the principal equestrienne of our circus. When we were at Tunbridge Wells I became acquainted with a gentleman who, though a clergyman, was very fond of innocent amusement, and always patronised any well-conducted circus company. He presented me with a bundle of tracts, and begged I would in my wanderings distribute them where I thought they might be useful. I took the parcel and directed it to old Clarke, having introduced a note in which I condemned his conduct, as an old man, bringing up his daughter to such a profession, displaying her beautiful limbs in silk tights and flimsy dresses, after the manner of the ballet girls so virtuously condemned by a late immaculate Lord Chamberlain, whose eyes were closed to the half-nude figures which appear at a court drawing-room. I expressed a hope that he would soon see his error and amend his ways. This note was conveyed to him in the dressing-room by a boy. Clarke came to me in great wrath, and asked me to read the letter. At that day's performance a gentleman, dressed in black, with white cravat and general clerical appearance, was seated in the boxes. So I told Clarke that I believed he was the person who had given the parcel to the boy. Now, Clarke was a man of violent passions, and indulged in the strongest expletives. The words were scarcely off my tongue before he rushed from the dressing-room tent, with the bundle of tracts under his arm and the open letter in his hand, placed himself in front of the astonished clergyman in the boxes, and yelled out in a paroxysm of rage, "I'll tell you what it is, Mr. Parson, I neither want your tracts nor your notes; and if you'll take my blessed daughter with you, and make her into a preacher, I think she'll be a jolly sight better off than she is now; and she'll have less danger and nothing to do but jaw for her money." By this time a crowd had assembled; and fearing the affair might become serious I informed Van Amburgh that old Clarke was at it again. So by the aid of two or three canvas men the infuriated father was removed, and after an apology from Mr. Van Amburgh the outrage was condoned.

On the morning of our second day at Tunbridge Wells, the patronage was so great that all the seats provided were crowded to excess, and we had to borrow forms and settles from schools and hotels, in order to accommodate our extra visitors. We had also about fifty invalids wheeled in their bath chairs, forming a sort of inner circle in front of the general spectators. It was altogether a sight rejoicing the manager's heart. But, as "there's always a fly in the apothecary's pot," so some one must always be disagreeable. Such a person appeared in the shape of a doctor of the neighbourhood. He occupied three seats, sitting on one, resting his feet on another, and supporting his back by a third. Though many ladies were standing, he would not move an inch to accommodate them. Several of our attachés used their powers of persuasion in vain. Even on Mr. Van Amburgh himself politely requesting him to confine himself to his proper seat, he rudely refused to do so. Van Amburgh then came to me in the dressing-room, and said, "There's a well-dressed blackguard in the boxes who won't listen to reason. Whatever the consequences may be I wish you to remove him by force." Being then in the prime of my manly strength, I was nothing loth, and instantly undertook the task. I went up to him, and civilly requested him to remove his feet. I received a reply more emphatic than courteous. So I immediately seized him by the collar, and falling on my back, planted my feet in his stomach, still holding him, and made him perform a somersault over my head, when he lay some time in the sawdust to recover his breath. Then burst forth a storm of hissing and hooting, and it appeared that those who had been loudest in complaining of his conduct were most vehement in expressing their disapprobation of his forcible ejectment. During the storm I slipped away from the scene of action. The uproar continued till Mr. Van Amburgh was obliged to appear before them. In his blandest manner he inquired the cause of their displeasure. Twenty voices at once explained how badly the poor gentleman had been treated. "By whom?" said he. "By one of your servants, a tallish man with dark moustache." He replied, "If he is one of my servants he shall not disgrace the establishment a moment longer." One by one the members of the company who answered the description were brought before the audience. The first was Paul Masotta. "Oh no!" they cried, "not so stout a man as he." The next was Tom Nunn. "Is that him?" "No,' shouted they, "A dark man." And when they had inspected nearly all our moustached members, Mr. Van Amburgh was obliged to produce the real culprit. You can imagine the reception I met with. When silence could be obtained he said, "Are you not ashamed of yourself?" Of course I hung down my head, an attitude befitting the solemn occasion. "How much am I indebted to you?" he cried. "Ten pounds," said I; and he instantly paid me two £5 notes. Then seizing me by the back of the neck he kicked me through the crowd. Thus running the gauntlet I received severe punishment from them, and was finally landed outside the front entrance. I speedily returned by the back way to the dressing room, while Mr. Van Amburgh was called into the arena to receive three hearty cheers from the gentlemen and all manner of kind words from the ladies. He soon joined me in the dressing tent, and sent for two bottles of champagne to heal my wounds of mind and body. In less than half-an-hour I stood before the same audience disguised in my jester's costume, and was applauded to the echo. Little did they think they were laughing at the fun of the man they had just before expelled for his brutality.

A short time after this we visited Warminster, where one of the lionesses had cubs, a very fine litter of four. When they were about a month old we removed to Windsor. The Court was there, and I had the honour of being introduced to Her Most Gracious Majesty the Queen, Prince Albert, the Duke of Wellington, the royal children, and the then lords and ladies in waiting. We were performing on some waste land on what is called Batchelor's Acre. Our beloved Queen was in a delicate state of health, which rendered it impossible for her to visit any place of public entertainment; but through the Hon. Mr. Anson she intimated her desire to see the Shakesperian clown (the title I bore at the time), of whom she had heard so much during my stay at Windsor. So by the kind permission of Van Amburgh I attended at Windsor Castle. This was on the 19th of July, 1844. And as Her Majesty had expressed her regret that she was not well enough to visit the " dear little creatures," as she called the young lions, it was arranged by Van Amburgh, myself, and the equerries-in-waiting that I should take the cubs with me, to afford her the opportunity of seeing them. I had a very gracious reception from the Queen and the Prince Consort and a large party of distinguished visitors. The affability and grace of these exalted personages made a deep impression on me. It might be copied by some of our grocers and muffin-bakers to their great improvement, and to the comfort of others surrounding them. The first word from Her Majesty inspires you with confidence to reply, as if you were addressing an equal, not forgetting the sense of duty due to her greatness and goodness.

At the fall of the year we visited Cambridge, where I soon became a favourite. But the principal attraction could scarcely be called legitimate, for the chief part of my entertainment was extracted from me by rather a curious process. The undergraduates were in the habit of congregating in large numbers, and generally contrived to hire some one to hiss me on my first appearance in the ring; not out of disrespect, but merely to draw me out. But I always managed to retaliate so powerfully upon the aggressor as to render him perfectly ridiculous. At length the consequences of disapprobation became so well known that when any of the youngsters said to a bystander, " I'll give you halfacrown to hiss Wallett," the reply was, " You hiss him yourself, and see what you'll make out of it." The Vice-Chancellor ordered us to remove from the town, according to powers exercised by him from time immemorial; but through the kindness of a friend I obtained a copy of the Act of Parliament from which these powers were derived, and discovered a vital flaw in it. Though the Act empowered the University authorities to prohibit any entertainment during term time, and they could obtain the conviction of trespassers, there was no mode specified for enforcing the penalty. So we remained in spite of the Vice-Chancellor and his army of proctors, till we were ready to go, and after that, to show that we could stay if we willed it. This was a grand discovery for circus people; for the good people of Cambridge may be numbered with the best supporters of amusements to be found in any town of its size in England. Ever since this time the town has been well entertained; for it is only necessary to pay the usual compliment to the mayor, and the arbitrary power of the Vice-Chancellor may be set at nought.

I remained with Van Amburgh till the end of my engagement with much comfort, receiving considerable emolument.

I next joined Mr. Edwin Hughes, of the Mammoth Circus, in which I was principally engaged as an artist. I then designed the first and best of all the ornamental carriages that ever travelled with circus tents. The great lion carriage drawn by elephants was my production. The enormous pictorial carriages, with rich carving and gilding, were my original design. The noble colossal carriage called the "Egyptian Dragon Chariot," which cost £750 in building, and was drawn by camels, and the harness and all the trappings, were also made from my patterns. This carriage was built by Messrs. Holmes, of Derby, coach builders to Her Majesty, from my sections and elevations, and under my personal superintendence. Thus I became the humble means of building for the proprietor a colossal fortune. Of course I received the salary agreed upon; but the liberal manager was so delighted with the elegance of the carriages and their wonderfully attractive power over the public, that in the exuberance of his gratitude he made me a present of a new suit of clothes. Three years after I received a county court summons from the tailor, and had to pay his bill myself.

After remaining with the circus some time, I went to Dublin, to join Batty, who then occupied the Music Hall in Abbey Street. On my way I stayed a night in Manchester, where Batty had another circus. I was dressed in a neat suit, with light coloured scarf, silk umbrella, and black kid gloves, not wishing to be recognized. I paid my money at the door, and entered the boxes. When I went in, a rider, Tom Lee, was performing on horseback. I had not been seated five minutes before he fell off, and dislocated his shoulder. I instantly sprang into the arena, had him conveyed to the dressing-room, cut off the dress from the injured arm, and ordered him a stiff glass of brandy and water. Off went my coat, and with the assistance of the bystanders I set his shoulder before inflammation could commence. It was not till the patient had his glass of brandy and water to restore him, his temples bathed with cold water, his shoulder properly bandaged, and his lower arm strapped across his body, and everything requisite had been done for him—it was not till then that Robert Smith, the ring-master, exclaimed, "Well, I'm sure that's no doctor; that must be Mr. Wallett." Then came thanks and congratulations, and expressions of gratitude from the man restored by my promptitude and energy.

Next morning I started for the Irish metropolis. During the season there, news arrived that Astley's was burnt down. Batty started for London by the first steamer, made arrangements to rebuild Astley's Theatre, and returned to Dublin with great exultation. When he appeared before the company he told them, "Thirty years ago I said I would one day be master of Astley's, and I shall never die till I'm Lord Mayor of Dublin." This last prediction was never verified. He made a princely fortune at Astley's, trading on the character that Ducrow had given it. He retired, and left it to Cooke, who exhausted the little vitality that Batty had left in it, until one of the most prosperous theatrical properties in the world sunk into irreparable ruin.

It was in Dublin that I first set up a horse and carriage. On my first ride out I met Batty. Of course I was delighted with my new turn-out, and anticipated a world of comfort from it. I pulled up to receive the greeting of the manager; when to my surprise he said, "Now, young man, you're just getting into trouble." I said, "I beg your pardon, I thought I was just getting into comfort." "No," said he, "a man's comfort is at an end when he has more property than he can look after himself." I thought it very absurd at the time; but hundreds of times afterwards, when owning a large stud of horses, spread all over a town, in every conceivable kind of stable, with mouldy hay and short measured corn, tended or untended by an army of drunken grooms, his words were borne upon my mind with great weight. They were, alas! too true.

About this time the first Agricultural Exhibition took place at Oxford, and the principal part of our troupe was taken to a new circus, erected in St. Giles's. I was left behind with a few people and two or three horses, to manage the Dublin business. It soon got mooted abroad that all the horses and most of the artists were gone, and of course our patrons dropped off in a corresponding ratio. So I received orders to take steamer to Liverpool, and join my comrades at Oxford. On our arrival at Liverpool we put up the stud at Lucas's Stables, near the amphitheatre then under the management of Mr. Copeland, one of the most honourable and kind-hearted of his class, whom I happened to meet at the stables. There was a great meeting at the time in Liverpool, but scarcely any amusements were provided. He inquired, "What are you doing here?" I told him I was managing for Batty, and just passing through the town with ten horses and a few performers. Said he, "You are the very man I want." So after some negociation, I agreed to open two days after with my small stud at the Amphitheatre, Mr. Copeland finding gas, building, printing, and band, and sharing the gross proceeds nightly with me, for the use of my troupe. There were no telegraphs then, so it was more difficult than it is now to find any one who had a desire to keep out of the way. Therefore as I had arranged the business without the knowledge of my principal, I resolved to see it through on the same condition. The speculation succeeded. My share for the first week amounted to nearly £200, none of which I remitted, neither did I send a line to my employer. He came in search, and on the Wednesday in the second week found us in Liverpool. When I handed him over upwards of £200, after paying all expenses, my services was rewarded with a blackguarding which none but he and a friend of his at Norwich were capable of giving. He told me he did not know whether he ought not to transport me, for using his property without his permission. However he allowed me to complete the engagement, and then started me for Oxford. I found, on receiving my next week's salary, that in gratitude for the enterprise which had just put £250 in his pocket, he had charged me double the contract price for bringing my horse and carriage to Liverpool. That night, after helping some of the Oxford collegians to take down the sign from the circus, on which was inscribed "William Batty, licensed to sell ale and porter, to be drunk on the premises," and carefully fixing it over the gate of one of the colleges, I threw up my engagement in disgust.

For a few days I amused myself with Pablo Fanque fishing in the Isis. Pablo was a very expert angler, and would usually catch as many fish as five or six of us within sight of him put together. This suggested a curious device. You must know that Pablo is a coloured man. One of the Oxonians, with more love for angling than skill, thought there must be something captivating in the complexion of Pablo. He resolved to try. One morning, going down to the river an hour or two earlier than usual, we were astonished to find the experimental philosophic angler with his face blacked after the most approved style of the Christy Minstrels.

I remained in Oxford till Pablo's benefit came on, when I appeared for that night only, and delivered a mock electioneering speech. In it I proposed to solve the vexed question of freemen's right to vote for the county as well as for the city. I had primed myself with facts and figures, had compared the number of freemen with the number of acres of freehold land belonging to the corporation, and consequently their property, and was able to show that there was land enough, in fact more than twice enough, to constitute each freeman a forty-shilling freeholder. This I intended for a joke, but it turned out something better—it was good law. Some ten or fifteen years afterwards, when the question came before a high tribunal, the judge came to the same decision that I had delivered in jest.

It was a great night. After my speech I was carried off to the hotel, where a splendid supper was spread, to which all the members of our troupe were invited. I recollect there was a great titter round the table, when a gentleman asking Lavator Lee, one of our company, to take wine with him, received the reply, "No, thank ye, sir, I'm drinking beer." After the usual toasts, and "He's a jolly good fellow," at least twenty times over, and repetitions of the resolution "We won't go home till morning," our party separated in great hilarity. It was my last night at the circus, and also that of Pablo, who left Batty to start an establishment of his own, which, after chequered fortunes, he still maintains.

After leaving Oxford, I went to Wakefield, Yorkshire, to join Pablo Fanque, who had erected a fine circus in Wood Street. Here I passed through one of the most severe trials of my professional life. A christening party, consisting of a young father and mother, with their little babe, and its old grandmother, were finishing the day at the circus. During the time I was in the ring, the old lady appeared to be in an ecstacy of enjoyment—so much so, that her hearty laughter attracted the attention of the whole audience and myself. But her laughter suddenly ceased, and her head fell back. I felt convinced that something serious had happened. So I stepped into the pit, took the old lady in my arms, and carried her into the lobby. I sat down on the steps, with the old lady on my knee, when she lifted her head, gave a gentle sigh, her head fell back on my shoulder, and her dear spirit had fled. I carried her body across to the Woodman Hotel, kept by Mr. Briggs, where a coroner's inquest was afterwards held. When I returned to the circus, I found they had not proceeded with the entertainment, but had stopped where I left them. Oh, what a difficult task it was to speak to the audience on the awful event that had occurred! To treat the subject with due solemnity, and yet to show the folly of grieving overmuch for what is inevitable. As each one could say

"I know that somewhere in the dark,
 The Shadow sits and waits for me."

The occurrence has never been forgotten by me, nor by the relatives of the old lady. Many years after, a middle-aged man, with his son, a grown man, waited upon me during a subsequent visit to Wakefield. He said, "You'll not remember me, sir, I am the son of the woman you carried out of the ring here, many years ago. Whenever I see your name announced, if within a day's walk, I come to see you. This is my son, the child we were christening on that day; and I've taught him to love you as I and his dear mother do."

I next visited Leeds with Pablo Fanque. I had become a popular favourite, and crowded houses nightly were the result of the announcement of my name. So much so, that on my benefit night at the circus in King Charles'-croft, when the house was crowded to excess, there were thousands outside, unable to gain admission. All went on well till about the middle of the entertainment, when, with a tremendous crash the gallery fell down, throwing several hundred people into a heap, mingled with broken timbers, but fortunately without loss of life to the spectators. My wife and Mrs. Pablo were seated together in the pay office beneath the falling mass. Mrs. Wallett happened to be sitting upright, and was knocked down by the timbers. She received some injury, but was not dangerously hurt. But poor Mrs. Pablo, who was looking over the front of the money-taking place, was struck by a falling beam, and killed on the spot. In the confusion that followed, some vile thief stole her watch from her side, and her box containing upwards of £50, the takings of the evening. The accident is thus described in the History of Yorkshire:—

Saturday night, the 18th March, 1848, a serious and fatal accident occurred at the circus of Mr. W. Darby, alias Pablo Fanque, King Charles'-croft, Leeds. It was the benefit night of Mr. W. F. Wallett, the clown; and the circus, consisting of a temporary wooden structure, was crowded in every part. The pit, which contained more than six hundred persons, fell with a tremendous crash, precipitating a great number of people into the gallery adjoining the front of the pit, but on a lower level. A many others fell into the lobby, and some out at one side, for the weight of the falling timber, and the people together, had burst out a portion of the side of the circus nearest to Land's-lane. Mrs. Darby and Mrs. Wallett were both in the lobby at the time of the occurrence. They were both knocked down by the falling timber; two heavy planks fell upon the back part of the head and neck of Mrs. Darby, and killed her on the spot. Mrs. Wallett, besides a many other persons, received bruises and contusions, but the above was the only fatal accident. The unfortunate woman was interred at the Woodhouse cemetery, where a monument records the melancholy event as follows:—

"Sacred to the memory of Susannah Darby, aged 47 years, the beloved wife of William Darby, equestrian manager, professionally known as Pablo Fanque. Her death was occasioned by the falling of a portion of the circus, erected in King Charles'-croft, on Saturday, the 18th of March, 1848.

> To God's decree we mortals all must bend,
> 'Thy will be done,'—our best and only friend.
> My soul, by thy commands, is borne away
> To realms of light and never-ending day.
> Torn from this world, and from my husband dear,
> Pity my fate, and drop a silent tear.

Her bereaved and afflicted husband caused this monument to be erected."

I next joined Mr. James Ryan, at Nottingham. His establishment appeared then on its last legs, for the bailiffs took possession that very day; and, to mend the matter, the bandsmen struck because their salaries were not paid. So I had to play clown and music too. In fact, I was the leader of the band at one time, for during the performance of Charles Adams (commonly called Finney) on the tight rope, I got into the gallery, and whistled a tune in which the gods joined with all gusto. Whistling is dry work, but luckily I had seated myself beside one of the gods who was amply supplied with nectar. He had a large jug of good Nottingham ale, with which I could wet my whistle whenever I had two bars' rest. The deities had ejected the bailiff in the early part of the evening, who, in his sudden departure, had left his stick behind, which served me as a bâton to conduct my windy orchestra.

The concluding piece was George and the Dragon. In the palace scene there were old Buck the King, Mrs. Field the Princess, four or five ladies and courtiers, who were closely grouped on a large packing-case that represented a throne, and poor Bill Davies, whose grave I lately saw at New Orleans. The princess was a large, stout, coarse woman, fuller of gin than grief; and when George came to receive the victor's crown from the hands of the fair princess, she entirely forgot what she had to do. Upon George remonstrating with her, she gave him a blow that sent the champion of Christendom reeling. Poor Bill was not the best tempered man that ever lived. This was an indignity he could not brook. He did not strike the princess, but gave her a push that was anything but gentle. The packing-case or throne, not having a spare inch of room upon it, in falling back she upset the Egyptian court, including old Buck the King, who all rolled in admirable confusion in the sawdust together. This brought the entertainment to a sudden conclusion; ended the piece, my engagement, and the management.

I was next engaged at Astley's Amphitheatre, London. Though Tom Barry, as clown, held undisputed sway here, I soon made my mark. It was not long before Barry became very jealous, and demanded that he should have the choice of the acts in the circus. Thus I must go only into what he thought proper. But Batty, who was a very straightforward man in some things, said to him, "That won't do, Mr. Tom, you've been master here long enough. You've time out of mind gone to races and fights, with your name on the bill for long parts and for clown, and never came near the place at all. Besides, you've said a hundred times you could bottle all the clowns in the world; and you've got a first rate opportunity of proving it by bottling Wallett." A piece called "The Arab and his Steed" had been in rehearsal some weeks. My part was a very subordinate one. But Barry's was the cream of the whole drama, with the exception of the Arab himself, played by John Dale, of Drury Lane. Barry's part of Barney Bralagan was a rollicking, dancing Irishman, with several songs and parts of duets. As I had attended all the rehearsals, and have a very retentive memory, I knew every word, song, and note of music long before Barry did. But of this he was not aware, or he would not have acted so foolishly as he did. For on the Saturday night previous to the Monday on which the part was to be produced, he waited upon Mr. Batty again, to tell him that if he could not have his choice of acts in the ring, he should not appear again; thinking that he was indispensable, and had the management in his power. Batty said he would take an hour to consider the matter, and let him know. The stage manager, Mr. T. Thompson, the renowned pantomimist, came to me, wishing to know whether, if I had the manuscript that night, I could get up in the part for Monday. Knowing that Barry had behaved so underhandedly towards me, I replied, I would endeavour to do so, as if I had still to learn the part, though I was dead-letter perfect in it. A kind good woman, Mrs. Johnson, the singing chambermaid of the establishment, gave me every assistance, and my dear friend, the late John Cooke, leader and composer, devoted his Sunday afternoon to practising Mrs. Johnson and myself in the music. Of course when Barry waited upon the manager for his ultimatum, he received the startling intelligence that his resignation was accepted. I read my part from the manuscript at the rehearsal on Monday, and got through it with a very bad grace, not even rehearsing the music, but saying it would be all right, "At night we'd manage it." In fact, I appeared so ignorant of the part, and so careless of the weight of responsibility upon me, that poor Thompson was in a fever. He told me, when the performance was over, that he expected I should have been the cause of the piece being damned, and that he had several times tried to find Mr. Batty, in order to persuade him at any cost to get Barry to return. The piece went off swimmingly. All our duets were encored. The whole was a great success. I played the part every night for a year, and during that time Barry was never once demanded.

By this time I had saved some money. So I invested it by opening two cigar divans that were then unequalled, and have never been surpassed for beauty of design and elegance of appointment by any in the metropolis.

Mr. Hughes visited Batty during my engagement, and obtained permission for me to play a fortnight with him at Birmingham. He asked my terms, and I agreed to go down to receive as my salary one night's gross receipts each week any night he thought proper. So I went, and when I inquired about my benefit, I heard with surprise that I must take it on Saturday evening. This was a night on which they had never performed, and on which there had never been any theatrical, concert, or other entertainment in the town for fifty years. When my bills were issued those who knew me thought I must be drunk, and those who did not thought I must be mad. But I persevered, and took infinite trouble to let it be generally known how I had been outwitted. In fact by the end of the week I found myself a martyr, and had the sympathy of the town as an injured man. The dear Brums rallied round me, and I had £84 in the house on my first night, and a very good house on the following Saturday. Mr. Hughes then found that Saturday nights might be made to pay, so he determined to open on that night for the remainder of the season. Benefits were coming on, and it so happened that the two clowns of the establishment drew two Saturdays for their benefits. For which blessing I doubt they gave me hearty thanks, as the cause of their unfortunate failures. However, Saturday performances became institutions, and all companies have acted here on these nights, which have proved the best in the week.

After my return to Astley's, Thompson withdrew from the management, and Wm. Broadfoot re-occupied that position, which he had held many years. He was the best stage manager for spectacles that ever lived in our time—except his great original master, Ducrow—but a man of irritable temper, and a great tyrant. However he was well matched with a noble band of irreconcileables. Poor Ben Crowther, Tom Lee, little Harvey the dancer, and, though last not least, myself. During the second week of his management he compelled us to rehearse a piece over and over again till it became unendurable: when a stuffed Astleyan cannon-ball came into violent contact with his head, and prostrated him on the floor. He stamped, he raved, and offered a reward of two pounds to any one who would betray the projector. So I came forward, and promised faithfully to reveal the culprit if the money was paid down at once. Mr. Batty was sent for, informed of the matter, and agreed to advance the two pounds, which he did. Broadfoot handed me the money, and then said "Who is the ruffian that threw the cannon ball?" I told him I did, and quietly pocketing the money, walked from the stage. According to the printed rule of the establishment the fine

G

for larking at rehearsals was only ten shillings, so I could well afford to pay the fine. With the remaining thirty shillings I treated the irreconcileables to a good dinner, where we drank in his absence the health of William Broadfoot, Esq., the founder of the feast.

It was near Christmas; and with a new spectacle and pantomime we were kept at rehearsal from ten in the morning till four in the afternoon, and sometimes till the curtain had to be dropped to admit the audience. Those who lived at a distance had frequently no time to go home to refresh themselves before the commencement of their evening duties. But this was not enough for our exacting manager. Perhaps to be revenged upon the malcontents, he actually called the reading of a new piece on the morning of Christmas Day, to prevent us enjoying our Christmas dinner, a privilege enjoyed by nearly all Her Majesty's subjects, not excepting paupers and convicts. On the arrival of the corps dramatique they found everything in apple-pie order. The stage covered with green baize, the curtain down, forms arranged across the front of the stage, and at the back was a table covered with red cloth, two silver candlesticks with lighted candles, the important manuscript, a bottle of water and a tumbler, and all requisites for a long reading. The border lights were burning, a pair of flats were placed on each side, enclosing the stage like a room, and giving it a very cosy appearance. But a wonderful pantomimic transformation was at hand; for my troupe had been stealthily but surely at work. The forms had cords attached to each of their legs. Those in the front had the ropes passed under the curtain into the orchestra, where we had two grooms placed waiting for a signal previously arranged. All the others, and the table and chair intended for the reader, were similarly prepared, the lines leading under flats where we had some insubordinate supers to act as our emissaries. Our holiday manager, got up for the occasion regardless of expense, took his seat behind the wax candles. The ladies and gentlemen were all seated around him, and even the troupe of `irreconcileables were present to a man. The seat of honour immediately faced the reader of the drama. Everything went smoothly till the end of the first scene, when a loud cough was heard; and lo! the principal actors, the leading actress, the singing chambermaid, the old man, the heavy old woman, the first and second low comedians, and the stage manager himself were suddenly overthrown. For at the cough, at least twelve pairs of willing arms pulled so energetically at the cords that all the forms, the table, and chairs, were upset with all that were thereon. There arose a chorus of screams and laughter, varied by the rank blasphemy of the enraged manager. During this time a messenger had been sent to one of our more distant agents, who not hearing the signal had failed to act in concert with his brother conspirators. Receiving the message he instantly jumped off his seat on the gas-meter and turned off the gas, thus further confounding with darkness the confusion on the stage. The baffled reader, rolling up his manuscript, made a hasty retreat, during which, dark as it was, he received many striking proofs of our appreciation of his benevolent intentions. We went our way rejoicing, to spend the festival day in a more fitting manner.

The next piece we brought out was an adaptation of a

French spectacle, called "The Devil's Horse." I had a capital part in that. The piece was brought out in the depth of winter, and Astley's is one of those theatres where no one was ever known to be suffocated for want of ventilation. The principal feat in my part, in the first scene, was sitting at a table, consuming a basin of pea soup that was provided nightly by old Mrs. Fleming, at the stage door. Jem Harwood was leading man at that time; and one night when there was a very slack house, and we thought the stage manager was napping somewhere, Harwood, attracted by the savoury smell of my soup, came up to the table, during my absence in front of the stage, and drank half of it. By way of retaliation, I took up a plate and broke it over the eminent tragedian's head. For this offence I was fined a week's salary, which I determined not to pay, and managed it thus. Mr. George Francis was treasurer. On Thursday afternoon I ran to him in a hurry and begged the loan of ten pounds till Saturday. He said very unfortunately he had not so much with him, but kindly promised to get it for me. He borrowed the money of Mr. Vickers, of the Rodney, in Westminster Bridge Road. On Saturday night Batty came to me on the stage, and said, "How is it, young man, you didn't come to the treasury to-day?" "Because I've nothing to receive; I borrowed the money of George Francis in the middle of the week to escape your iniquitous fine." He replied, "Well, never mind, it's all right, I can stop it next week." I told him he would never have the chance, for, as he was probably unaware, my six months' engagement terminated that very night. I accordingly left him, sold up my cigar divans, and quitted the metropolis in hope of more lucrative business in the provinces.

CHAPTER V.

"Everything by turns, and nothing long.'

DURING my lengthened sojourn in London, I purchased the plant of a soda-water manufacturer, comprising the most improved machinery at that time invented for making aërated waters. This was some years previous to the introduction of my invention of the self-charging process, which has been for years successfully carried on at the Crystal Palace, having been introduced there by Mr. Fox, of Manchester. I worked my own invention at a manufactory I established in Carlton Street, Nottingham, where I soon made a first class trade. But unfortunately, I was my own town traveller, and as I did a great part of my business with hotel-keepers and publicans, I was led into considerable temptation. For in order to obtain and maintain a connection, for three or four nights a week I considered myself obliged to take the chair at free-and-easys, birthday clubs, house-warming dinners, opening suppers, and to become a member of raffles for watches that wouldn't go, musical boxes that wouldn't play, and to respond to a multitude of other such calls, which, altogether, kept me from home till all hours of the night, injured my health, and drew me into loose ways. So I determined to retire from this ensnaring business. I soon had hosts of applicants, for it really was a prosperous and lucrative affair; but in spite of tempting offers, gratitude was the highest bidder. Some years previously, being very short of money, a dear friend of mine, a chemist and druggist in Clumber Street, Nottingham, now deceased, kindly proffered me a loan of £100 at a time when it was the means of saving me from great loss of property. I had been fortunate enough to repay him shortly after. Now my friend, at the time of the loan, was director of a banking company, which afterwards failed, and spread ruin around. He received rather more than his share of the calamity; for he lost all he had in the world. It was now my turn to befriend him; and as my trade was allied to his, I resolved to let him have it, subject merely to the broker's valuation, and to take his own time for payment. He was very successful in his trade, which I believe is still carried on by his son.

I then undertook the establishment and management of a circus of my own. I purchased horses, harness, wardrobe, and all requisites for a first class equestrian concern. I commenced my managerial career at Yarmouth, where I erected a very fine amphitheatre. The support I received was very meagre, for the entertainment was too good for the taste and capacity of the people. However, I secured the patronage of the mayor of the town, for whose night I had two bills printed on white satin, at a cost of three shillings each, one of which I sent to him, and the other to his maiden sister. On the morning of his worship's bespeak, a randan was heard at my door, and a high official of the police entered, and said he came with the mayor's compliments to secure places for the evening.

I was having breakfast at the time, but set my coffee aside, and allowed the toast to cool while I ran upstairs to get the plan of the box seats. Imagine my mortification when, upon inquiring the number his worship required, the policeman replied, "Two, at half-a-crown each." The disappointment and the spoiling of my breakfast so annoyed me, that I threw the tickets into the fire, and begged the officer to give my compliments to the mayor, and tell him to buy bloaters with his five shillings. As soon as my building at Colchester was completed, I bade adieu to the intellectual herring-catchers, with an earnest prayer that I might never again fall into their meshes.

I was well received and properly appreciated at Colchester. But here my old luck overtook me once more. The only architect I could engage was one named Fred James, a person upon whom very little reliance could be placed, and through his carelessness I came to grief. During the second night's performance a storm came up, and the greater part of the roof over the gallery was blown down upon the audience. Several were severely injured; two arms and one leg were broken, but there was no fatal casualty. This untoward accident, of course, destroyed all confidence in the security of the building, ruined the business, and involved me in law-suits that lasted two years. There was nothing for it but to retreat as soon as possible. So I went to Ipswich, to arrange for the erection of a circus there. Old Devonport, the father of the present great actress of that name, was the manager of the Theatre Royal here, and had just commenced his first season. When he discovered my intention, to prevent me from opposing him, he agreed to give me the use of his Theatre

Royal at Bury St. Edmunds rent free for two or three weeks, until I could erect a suitable building at Leicester. Before taking farewell of Colchester, I must record my thanks to Sir Harry Smith, his dear niece, and the whole family and other friends at Bearchurch Hall, who were my unfailing supporters.

I constructed a ring upon the stage at Bury St. Edmunds, and should have done extremely well, but was unfortunately compelled by my contract with Mr. Devonport to charge the old prices—four shillings to the boxes, two shillings to the pit, and one shilling to the gallery. This was at a time when nearly all the theatres in London were charging only half these prices. At length I was compelled to evade this contract, which was ruining my business, by admitting two persons for one payment. Thus I was able to keep the theatre open till the building at Leicester was completed. My worthy friend Mr. Devonport, was highly indignant at this evasion of our contract; at least, so report said, for I never saw him till seven years afterwards, when we met in Broadway, New York, when he was on a tour with his daughter. The weather was very hot, (and it can be hot in New York,) but my friend (whom Dickens has immortalized) was sweltering in an enormous blue military cloak. We recognised each other, and he said, "On this side of the water we are friends, but if ever we meet in old England again, John Doe and Richard Roe shall try the issue between us." He never lived to see the trial. May he rest in peace!

In a magnificent circus, erected in Market Street, Leicester, I opened an equestrian campaign. I received as much patronage as any other unfortunate manager that ever visited this unhappy town. Whatever took me there I cannot imagine; I must have been mad, for I had visited it many years before, with the great Ducrow in all his glory, with his dramatic and equestrian company from Astley's, and scenery and wardrobe, in an amphitheatre equal in size and beauty to any in Europe. We scarcely took as much money in a week as would pay one night's expenses. I visited it again with Mr. Cooke, sen., when his sons, Thomas, James, William, Henry, Alfred, and George, the whole family, with a stud of forty horses and all the novelties of the day, performed in a large building in Belvoir Street, where we many a time went through the entire performance to less than thirty shillings—the quadrupeds and bipeds of the establishment outnumbering threefold the audience. That was a fearful season. There were very heavy snow storms. A man stood at the corner of the building, selling pies, and stamping his toes to keep them from freezing. Every now and then, between the acts, we could hear his melancholy voice, which sounded like an utterance of our misery. He was crying "Orl ort," but in so dismal a tone that it sounded like a pious ejaculation of distress. The only respectable professional man I ever knew to live in Leicester was that highly cultivated musician, Henry Nicholson, Esq. He has lived there for years, but the reason is he does not get his living there. Every theatrical season in this town terminates in bankruptcy, and music halls have like success. A dirty penny show may exist in it, but no circus with a horse and a half. In fact, you may judge of the encouragement given to caterers for the public amusement, by the occasional appearance in the London "Era," of a communication from an intelligent correspondent, running thus: "Leicester—We have had no amusement here for a length of time. A good circus would do well. We should be happy to hear from Herr Mauss, Mr. Crouest, or Mr. Manley." I had, however, my kind friends at Leicester, few of whom now remain; and I must confess that I had a better season than I can remember any other manager to have had. In due time I bade adieu to my Leicester friends, assuring them that I would never again erect a circus within sound of a stocking-frame.

My next visit was to dear old Nottingham, where I was most kindly received. I did a great business here, and was honoured with the patronage of Lord Rancliffe, Sir Juckes Clifton, Bart., Colonel Wildman, Sir Harvey Bruce, — Carver, Esq., who was then mayor, and who favoured me with a flattering testimonial, and a letter of introduction to the mayor of Bradford, Titus Salt, Esq., to be used when I left Nottingham. I was presented with a splendid silver snuff-box at Malpas's Flying Horse Hotel, and patronised by the Anacreontic Society, the Senior Glee Club, Harmonic Society, Odd Fellows, Foresters, Druids, &c., and though last, not least, by "the Craft."

After an affecting farewell, I started for Bradford, where my introduction secured me a warm reception. Here I gave several benefits and large sums to the local charities, and one in aid of a library and reading room, for which I was presented with a testimonial on parchment, which I have always valued, and still retain.

The next performance was in Leeds, where I erected a building capable of holding three thousand persons, in Woodhouse Lane. It was a sad time; several banks broke, and, to add to the general panic, there was an outbreak of cholera so virulent that the mayor prohibited all fairs and feasts. I lost at this time several thousand pounds from the ruination of trade by the general depression, aggravated by the terrible epidemic. It became so bad that at last I determined to leave, and took the riding school at Huddersfield.

The builder of the circus at Leeds, Mr. East, whom I afterwards met in America, gave me every assistance in his power. One night, after the conclusion of the performance, we took down the gallery and pit, and packed them in waggons for removal to Huddersfield. The arrangements were hurriedly made and very incomplete, and unfortunately the elevations were not the same as at Leeds, where things had been made to fit properly. We opened to a very crowded house. The back of the gallery had been elevated too much, which threw the bearers of the seats out of the perpendicular. So when the audience began to move, as they do in showing approbation, the back seat of the gallery was pressed forward against the backs of the legs of the sitters on the seats before it; that again was pressed forward against the next seat, and so on to the very front. It was the work of an instant. Upwards of five hundred persons had their limbs jammed between the seats, all being as firmly locked as if they had been placed in the stocks. And you may be sure I did not get many expressions of gratitude out of my compressed friends. The performances were, of course, suspended. We had to begin at the top, and release the captives row by row, which occupied upwards of two hours; all this time those nearest the front suffered severely from the pressure of those behind. The disaster spoiled my prospects, and compelled me to move on.

Meanwhile, my architect, Mr. Fred James, was erecting a building at Burnley, Lancashire. I sent him word of the accident, and received a reply that I might come on immediately with the troupe, as the building would be ready on the following Saturday. So, under the pressure of circumstances, I left my dear and squeezed friends at Huddersfield, with a heavy heart and light purse. Judge my astonishment, on my arrival at Burnley after a long and wet journey, when I found no roof on the circus; for, owing to the cold and bad weather, the joiners had struck work. So I had to remain idle for two weeks and a half, while we got men from Manchester to complete the building, my expenses being upwards of £130 a week. At length we opened, but found that the worthy citizens of this place had more taste for thick beer, short pipes, and ha'porths of boiled peas, than for circus or any other amusements. No use remaining here—must move on, somewhere, anywhere, anywhere.

A building erected by Pablo Fanque was standing vacant in the Ship Yard, Wigan, which I rented. By this time the epidemic was at its height. Here it was terrible. I lived at the Buck-'ith-Vine, now called the "Clarence Hotel," and while sitting at breakfast on the second morning, I counted ten vans passing with the dead. The churches were open day and night. Naturally our business was wretched. On one occasion I gave out five hundred free admissions, and not more than twenty were presented.

Franconi's French troupe were performing in the old Free Trade Hall, Manchester, where he had been doing a first class business for upwards of four months. I went over, and made arrangements with him to bring the whole of my company from Wigan, and join him. So that we had double stud, double band, double company; and with my name and popularity at Manchester, the patronage was overwhelming. We were greatly assisted by Mr. James Hernandez, the great American rider, who here made his début before an English audience, and achieved a success unparalleled in the history of equestrianism. I was thus enabled to pay off many pressing debts, and large sums of arrears of salary to my company.

At the conclusion of the engagement with Franconi I purposed returning to Wigan till I could erect another circus. I had been staying with an old friend, Mr. Charles Cox, of the Theatre Royal Tavern, one of the most sterling friends it was ever my fortune to make. The horses, carriages, and company were all arranged at the side of the Theatre Royal, near his house, ready to start. When two or three of the performers, who had received a large proportion of the money due to them, waited upon me and demanded further payment. The first and rudest was Jack Russelli, who received a proper castigation for his ungrateful conduct. Several others followed suit, and met with a similar reception. I felt disgusted with them, knowing as they did that they had received the greater part of the money for which I had worked hard for years, and that if I had been content to have let management alone I might have pocketed several hundreds a-year, instead of wasting my valuable time and getting into debt. I went down stairs, and met the head groom, who said to me, " When shall you be ready to start, sir?" The reply was " Never again.

Ladies and gentlemen, all dismount." That being done, I placed a groom upon each carriage, and taking the leading one myself drove them back to the stables they had just left. I then jumped into a cab, went to Buckstone's Repository in Salford, and made arrangements to sell every thing off on the following Wednesday. Within a few hours the walls were placarded, " Sale by auction, forty circus horses, carriages, harness, wardrobe, and all requisites, without reserve." Thus ended my second experiment in management. The money realized by the sale helped to pay a few urgent claims, but others becoming equally pressing I had to part with almost every shilling I had. I was indebted to my friend Cox twenty-seven pounds, which he kindly allowed to stand over till I was able to pay, though he greatly needed the money at the time. I now formed the determination of going to America, if I could only find the means of getting there. I ran down to Leeds to see an old friend, Thomas Askwith, a printer, who had done my printing for twenty years, and made my design known to him. I then owed him about fifty pounds. He said to me, "Wallett, my boy, thou hast always paid me, and what I have thou hast helped to make for me. I certainly have not much; but if thou wantest to go to America, I'll lend thee £100 to enable thee. If God gives thee health and strength, thou wilt as surely pay me, as thou always hast done; but if thou stoppest here, and they put thee into jail, thou'lt not be able to pay either me or any body else." I took the money gratefully. I then obtained the protection of the Insolvent Court at Leeds, agreeing to pay £150 a-year to my creditors, and as much more as I could.

CHAPTER VI.

"I pass like light from land to land,
I have strange power of speech."
Ancient Mariner altered.

I LEFT Liverpool in the screw steamer Sarah Sands, with my wife, agent, and a man-servant who had been with me since he was a boy. After a voyage of eighteen days we took a pilot on board at Sandy Hook, who brought with him a file of New York papers, one of which nearly killed my hopes. For to my surprise and discomfiture I found that the only circus in New York had closed the previous Saturday. It was on Sunday night about eight o'clock when I landed at a wharf in the East River, leaving my wife on board. I had collected all the funds in our united possession, amounting to eighteen shillings, and with this sum I made my way to the Branch Hotel in the Bowery, then the grand rendezvous of the profession. The bar-room was crowded; and as I held my handkerchief to my face to escape recognition, I took a survey of the faces around me. I discovered lots of old friends known in Europe: Ned Derious, Van Amburgh, Mr. Titus, Gerald Quick, Dick Sands, Bobby Williams, Cadwallader, Tom Hyer, Dick Platt, Bill O'Dale, and others. When I had taken stock, I removed the handkerchief, and sung out, " I wish you all a merry Christmas." I was instantly recognized, and many voices cried out at once, "Why, here's Bill Wallett!" Then came hearty cheers, enough to shake the roof tree. Then followed shaking of hands enough to give me rheumatism in the shoulders for the rest of my life. I only wish that some of my countrymen who boast of English welcome and hospitality could have heard the fervent "God bless you" uttered by every tongue.

I soon forgot my cares and sorrows under such genial influences. Next day I went to a prosperous man, to whom I had been of some service in my native land, and in a straightforward manner stated my circumstances. He kindly offered me the shelter of his roof, and to supply me with all necessaries till an opening should occur. He was the only person who knew my condition. The circus which was closed had been erected by General Welch, the prince of all equestrians either at home or abroad. The winter was very severe. The circus was a long way from the city, near the Vauxhall Gardens, on the very site where the Bible Society's house now stands. The proprietor had been obliged to close it, on account of the sharp weather and consequent falling off of attendance. There was a jolly old Trojan named John Tryon, who has for the last thirty years provided a circus home in New York or Boston during each winter for those who are thrown out of employment at the end of the summer season. In fact, instead of calling his establishment a circus, it ought to be entitled "John Tryon's Refuge for the Destitute." It was he who first offered to take and open the circus, in order to give me an opportunity of appearing before a New York audience. But the dear friend with whom I lived urged upon me the policy of not being in too great a hurry, remarking that a week or two made no difference to him, and would be a great object in my engagements. Therefore, being independent for the time, I was not compelled to accept the first offer, but could wait to make my own terms, which I soon obtained. The great day of appearance arrived. It was a very fine morning, but about noon commenced the first and only real snow storm I had ever seen. It seemed to increase in density as evening approached. About six o'clock while we were at dinner, I had risen from the table several times to look through the blinds, and had seen the snow still coming down, and about knee-deep on the ground—I could not eat, but almost gave way to despair. I said to my wife, "It's of no use; we might as well give it up, our old fortune pursues us everywhere." But her cheering smile and words encouraged me. At that moment a knock was heard at the door. It was one of Mr. Tryon's sons, who came to tell me the house had long been full, and they wished me to come immediately, to commence an hour before the time announced. So I hurried away and found the house crowded in every part, and a thousand persons outside unable to gain admission. Every thing went off beautifully; and I received my share of the proceeds at the close of the performance. On my arrival home I counted out before the astonished eyes of my rejoicing partner 300 dollars, or £60 sterling for this first night's performance in New York.

I remained at New York some time with great success, and afterwards accepted an engagement under General Welch to open at the National Theatre and Circus, Chestnut Street, Philadelphia. Here I met with a reception surpassing even that at New York. I must here bear my testimony to the straightforward and manly dealing I experienced from the proprietor and his secretary, Mr. George Russell, from whom I always received the attention and kindness of brothers. To perpetuate the memory of the latter, I christened one of my children by his name. During my stay here I made arrangements to travel for six months the following summer with Mr. S. B. Howes, under canvas, through the States. I moreover purchased a small estate and built a house at Frankfort, near Philadelphia, and having sent for my father and mother from England, we were all comfortably settled at Vine Cottage. I was well treated by my brother performers, excepting one, a clown; but I forgive him, for I am sure his head and not his heart was in fault. This was proved, for shortly after he was pronounced insane, and eventually died in a lunatic asylum. My great success was too much for his weak brain, so he hired twenty or thirty loafers to hiss me out of the ring. I had made many kind friends in dear old Philadelphia, some of whom combined to defeat my jealous rival. His plot leaked out during the day that the interruption was to have been attempted, but as I lived five miles out of the city I was entirely ignorant of it till my arrival in the ring. My friends however had not been idle. Captain Peters and his brother Rex, who were the largest omnibus proprietors in the city, actually took their omnibuses off the road an hour before the usual time, and sent a hundred of their men to the circus. My appearance in the ring was greeted with a storm of disapprobation, when a pistol was fired from the boxes, as a signal to Peters's men, who were stationed all over the building. In a moment there were two or three at every malcontent, dragging him from his seat and roughly handling him, till nearly the whole gang were handed over to the police outside. Then my defenders returned, gave me three hearty cheers, and the performance proceeded till my next act, when one of the killers who had been overlooked in the general clearance, shouted out, "Why, Wallett, they said you had run away!" I walked right up to him and said, "Run away! I run away! I'll let you know that the same blood circulates in my veins as in those of the men who landed on the rock of Plymouth, and fought at Bunker's Hill, and do not know how to run." Cheers which long made the dome echo followed, and before the vibration ceased my friend was drawn out of the crowd as cleanly as a tooth by an experienced dentist. this was the first and only annoyance I experienced during the many years I spent in America.

My next visit was to Boston, Massachusetts, with my old friend Tryon again, at the old Federal Theatre. Here my success was equal to that in New York or Philadelphia. We had only three horses in the establishment, Lady North, Old Mex, and Washington. They belonged to S. B. Howes, and all had the camel itch. Jem Nixon was equestrian manager. To make out our entrées our manager had to hire horses from livery stables, and as there had been a heavy fall of snow, and horses were in great demand for sleighing, we sometimes had to put off our entrées till nearly ten o'clock at night, waiting for the horses' return from their day's work. Their legs were hastily washed, and their sweating and stained bodies covered with rich velvet, bedizened with spangles, really cut a very respectable figure. The first night we opened, when Billy Nicholls, who was very hard of hearing, was riding Old Mex, the ring on the stage had not been completed till a late hour, so neither horses or men had had any chance of practice. The horse being very fresh through want of exercise, every time Billy leapt over an object and alighted on the horse's back, he was kicked up into the air. This occurred time after time. Neither horse nor rider seemed inclined to give in. At length it became tedious, and the audience showed their disapprobation by hissing and hooting vigorously. After explaining the difficulties under which we laboured, I begged them to extend their indulgence to the rider, adding "You may as well do so, and save your breath; your noise is entirely thrown away, he is as deaf as a stone." After the first night every thing went on right, and crowded houses nightly rewarded our exertions.

At the close of the season at Boston I went to Baltimore, to Front Street Theatre, where again I had a favourable gale. The agreement I made with Mr. Howes specified that I should commence my summer tour on the first of May, but there was a clause that I should join at any time previous, upon receiving a fortnight's notice in writing. Mr. Howes had engaged Mons. Madame and Benoit Tournaire to come out from Europe, with their whole family and stud of horses. Now it happened that they arrived in New York much sooner than they were expected, and as their salaries commenced on landing it was the interest of the manager to open as early as possible. So he sent me a letter desiring to know my terms for coming to New York for a month. I referred him to the clause in the agreement in such case made and provided, but this did not satisfy him. He repeated the inquiry; I repeated my reply. At length I received an unconditional order to join at New York. The terms of our agreement for the summer were a good salary, a horse and carriage to be kept for me, and all my hotel expenses paid. So upon arriving at New York I waited upon the acting manager, Mr. Jem June, and inquired on what hotel I was billeted. He replied no arrangements had been made, and I might go where I pleased. So of course I went to Florence's in Broadway, where I remained for a month, performing at Eighth Street Circus with Howes and the Tournaire troupe. On our removal to Brooklyn, Long Island, opposite New York, I obtained my hotel bill, and presented it to Mr. June, who refused to pay it, stating that my hotel expenses were only to be paid during the travelling season. After a long war of words, and threats to withdraw my services, we agreed upon the principle of payment. Then came taxation of costs, and higgling over sundry items. I had had extra breakfasts sometimes and extra suppers of oysters. (Splendid oysters they were: I wish I had some now, I would show what I thought of their delicate flavour.) These were objected to; but I replied, "It is not nominated in the bond how many meals I am to have per diem." "No," said the legal manager, "nor is it stipulated how many acts you are to appear in each performance either; and if you eat as often as you like, I'll make you act as often as I like." So my colleague, Bobby Williams, who was engaged as second clown to assist me, got a fortnight's notice to quit, and the whole of the clowning was thrown upon me. Thus you see I had made a pretty rod for my own back.

Our day performances in New York and its vicinity were generally well patronized by theatricals, equestrians out of employ, nigger singers, and various other classes of dead heads. So our first performance in Brooklyn was to a crowded house, the principal elements consisting as described. I commenced by appealing to the sympathies of the free list, begging them to endeavour to laugh at the jokes if possible, and to be very careful not to laugh at the wrong time. For I assure my readers, that those who frequent theatres for nothing are more difficult to please than the kindly public who fairly pay for admission. I had to appear six times as clown that afternoon. And still worse; for when I thought my labours were finished, I was told by Mr. Nixon, the equestrian manager, that I must play the comedy part in the after-piece called, "Jack the Giant Killer." This piece was really well put before the public, and must have cost a considerable amount of money. We had a splendidly modelled castle, single-headed and double-headed giants, male giants and female giantesses that swallowed live children—altogether a very complete production. After dressing for my part I was furnished with a huge wooden sword. I had no rehearsal, and was therefore ignorant of the action of the drama. On the entrance of a ponderous giant with his massive club I stood upon my defence, and fought him like a man and a hero. With the first blow I scalped him; my sword then went through his eye, and out at the back of his head. The next severed the head from his shoulders, and sent his trunk rolling in the sawdust. I then belaboured his body with my sword till the basket work flew in a thousand pieces, and then in great terror appeared "Snug the joiner," a canvas man called Long Jem, who crept from the interior of the giant to the extreme delight of the audience, and made rapid tracks towards the dressing room. The other giants shared the same fate one by one, without the slightest assistance from my friend Jack the Giant Killer. Having despatched the giant horde, I next took a flying leap on to the top of the mimic castle. My weight crushed it to atoms, and I fell buried in the ruins. This concluded the morning performance. On arriving in the dressing-room I found Mr. Howes waiting for me. With pale lips trembling with passion, he said, " Is that the way to fight giants?" When I coolly replied, "No, sir, it is not. I knew how to fight giants before you were born. The proper mode is to dig a large pit, then cover it over with light boughs and twigs hidden with sods and grass, and when pursued your light form passes over this in safety, but the giant's great weight breaks all beneath him, and he is buried in the pit. Then you throw a noose over his neck, properly secure him, and despatch him at your leisure. But you know, Mr. Howes, the giants came upon me so suddenly I had no time to dig a pit, and no spade or tools, as you forgot to supply them. If you had only told me beforehand that they were only paper masks and canvas work, with a labourer inside each, I should not have been so frightened at their appearance, and performed such havoc as I did in my own defence." He said no more, but I knew what he thought. He only wished I had been a giant and he Jack for a quarter of an hour. In that case I feel convinced this description would never have been written. At the evening entertainment there was a fresh programme printed, and my friend Bobby Williams took his share in the various acts in the ring. I had finished some time before the after-piece came on, and had dressed myself ready, sword in hand, prepared for another onslaught amongst the Brobdignagians. Luckily, as the piece was intended to conclude the entertainment every day during the season, the manager, to provide for wear and tear, had two sets of giants and properties made at the same time. He came in, saw me ready equipped, gave a sardonic grin, and hastily retired. Shortly after, Mr. Nixon appeared, and said, "Mr. Wallett, I shall not trouble you to appear in the after-piece, as I think Bobby Williams can fight giants much better than you can." In a day or two a flag of truce appeared, and we came to a proper understanding. And though I have served Mr. Howes as clown for many years we never had any difference afterwards. In fact, he placed so much confidence in me, that during one of his visits to England, he fitted out one of the finest establishments that ever travelled in Europe, called it "The Wallett Show," and conducted everything in my name, to our mutual satisfaction and profit.

After travelling with different companies through the eastern States, I went to join Ballard and Bailey's American Circus at Kingston, Canada. I travelled with this establishment to Montreal, Quebec, and all the Canadian cities, returning to the United States by the river St. Lawrence, the Thousand Islands, visited the Falls of Niagara, Lakes Ontario, Erie, Michigan, and Superior, and proceeded to Milwaukie, Chicago. Here I received letters of engagement from Dr. Spaulding, of Spaulding and Rogers' Floating Palace Circus. So I started off by canal across the State of Illinois, to La Salle, on the river Illinois, whence I took steamer for St. Louis, on the Mississippi. There I met Vanordan, the manager for Spaulding and Rogers, who received me in the most hospitable manner. I remained with him about a week, before we could get any tidings of the company; for the Floating Palace had struck on a sand bank in the Mississippi, and was there detained. I shall never forget my astonishment upon first viewing her (or it). It was a regular circus, equal in size to the largest that are erected in England, built on an enormous flat-bottomed vessel. A really splendid amphitheatre, with boxes, pit, and gallery, capable of seating nearly three thousand persons. There were stabling for thirty horses, and sleeping apartments for the artists, crew, and servants. She was towed along from town to town by an enormous high pressure steamship, visiting all the chief places on the Upper and Lower Mississippi, the Illinois, the Missouri, and their numerous branches. On one occasion, they actually towed her from New Orleans, out of the mouth of the Mississippi, the Belize, into the Gulf of Mexico, where, a storm coming on, she was nearly lost, but happily arrived safely by way of the Bay of Mobile, at the city of Mobile, Alabama. The whole concern was admirably conducted. The advertising agent, in a small steamer called the Humming Bird, proceeded about a fortnight in advance of the company, arranging at the different landing-places for fuel for the steamer, fodder for the horses, and provisions for the company and attachés, and posting the bills to advertise our coming.

I remained with this company a considerable time; the members of the company vieing with each other in showing me kind attentions. I would here record the fact, which is contrary to the report of many, that I never was under any circumstances, or at any place, insulted, or even slighted by Americans, because I was an Englishman.

On the Floating Palace reaching the bank of the river, she was moored as near to the town as possible. Huge platforms were lowered from the side, which formed an entrance portico to the different parts of the circus; the whole most brilliantly illuminated. We generally finished our entertainment in the southern and south-western portions of the country about nine in the evening, and were then accustomed to enjoy ourselves in the cities, till the bell rang all aboard. This reminds me of the following incident. The conductors of railway trains in America hold a somewhat different position to that of guards in this country. They collect money on the journey, and give tickets to the passengers. Immediately before starting from any station, the conductor runs along the platform, and cries out " All aboard !" and the train then starts. On one occasion the guard going his round observed, with the quick eye which practice alone can give, a passenger in a train of two or three hundred persons, who had not paid his fare. He inquired of the defaulter, an Irishman, " Where's your ticket, sir ?" Said Paddy, " Sure, I havn't got one, yer honour." " Where's your money ?" " Divil a red cent have I got." " I shall turn you out at the next station," was the reply. As soon as the train stopped, Paddy was rather roughly ejected. The conductor walked along the cars again, calling out as usual, " All aboard !" When the train had been some time in motion, he walked through the carriages, and, to his surprise, discovered the Irishman snugly seated in a corner. In a towering rage, he said, " Didn't I turn you out at the last station ?" The man replied, " To be sure ye did, yer honour; but I thought as I was a poor man your heart warmed towards me, and you'd altered your mind intirely; for didn't I hear ye call out 'All aboard!' and how the blazes could we be all aboard if I was left behind?" The conductor burst out laughing, and said, "All right, old fellow, you're good for a ride."

Our company at length reached New Orleans, and being the winter season, we quitted our floating for a fixed circus in the Third Municipality, known as the French Quartiére. We here came into opposition with Dan Rice, the great American clown, who treated me very kindly, notwithstanding he was at the head of the rival establishment. Our two circuses were close together, and I was on such friendly terms with the other company, that I one night ran out in my dress into the ring where Rice was performing. There we fraternised, and he introduced me to his patrons. From this moment I became a great favourite with the frequenters of both circuses. For Dan was a sort of martyr in the eyes of the New Orleans people; and it was believed that our proprietors, who were rich and powerful, had come on purpose to crush his company. In fact, the feeling rose to such a height that it was dangerous for our managers or any of their company to be recognized by the populace after dark. But though I made a lasting friend of Dan, and got into the good graces of the people, I incurred the displeasure of my employers. As we were not well supported, we soon left for Mobile, where I soon found to my cost, that the conduct of the managers was entirely changed, and they took every opportunity of showing their ill will.

Before leaving New Orleans, Dan kindly told me that I could at any time join him on the same terms I then received, to come when I pleased, and find a home with him. So I telegraphed to him that I should be at liberty on a certain day. The prompt reply was, "Come immediately; we have announced you." I went; and for a long time enjoyed much comfort and consideration from Rice, Mrs. Rice, and the manager, Henry Whitbeck. Dan and I played in the same circus to crowded houses. He played ring-master to me as clown in one act, and then we exchanged characters, and I was master of the ring to him. So pleasant was our association, that on leaving him he presented me with a valuable silver vase, which I still possess, and greatly prize.

Having been nearly a year away from my home and family, at Frankfort, I resolved to return. I took my passage in the steamer "Quaker City," from Mobile to Havanna, in Cuba, where I met Chinnicelli and an American troupe, at the Place of the Bull Fight. Here I had the honour of appearing before upwards of eighteen thousand people, including two entire regiments of the Spanish army, the governor-general of the island, and a brilliant staff. The brothers Hanlon, the premier acrobats of the world, were here. They had landed a few days before me, by a ship in which the master to whom they had been apprenticed, Mr. Lee, had died. I remained on the island about a month, wandering round the beautiful bay, visiting the tobacco and sugar plantations, the impregnable fort, Moro Castle on the heights commanding the entrance. After visiting Matanzas, Cardenas, and other places of interest, and after being sumptuously entertained by Signor and Signora — (late Mrs. John Gossen), at their princely residence, I bade adieu to my kind hosts and many friends made during my stay, and quitted the Queen of the Antilles by the Quaker City, on her next voyage from Mobile to New York.

The weather was intolerably hot, the thermometer ranging as high as 110° in the shade. When I got on board, I found the hurricane deck was covered with old Staffordshire pot crates, filled with oranges just gathered, and brought on board in baskets by negroes. The fruit was too ripe to be packed in boxes or stowed in the hold of the ship, and was placed thus to be exposed to the air. A great change soon came over us; for on the fifth day out, we suddenly altered our course to the northward, and ran out of the warm water of the Gulf of Mexico into the chilly Atlantic. Holding on our course, the intensity of cold seemed to increase every hour. Fires were lighted; trunks unpacked to get out warm clothing. "Steward, bring more blankets!" was the general cry. So great was the alteration of temperature, that on arriving at New York, seven and a half days after leaving the island, the thermometer had sunk to 15° below zero. It may be more readily imagined than described, how trying this was to the constitutions of many of us, who had been for a year or more in a climate in which white linen suits were the only wear. Landing at New York, the warm greetings I received soon made me forget the inclemency of the weather. After passing an hour or two with old friends, I left the city by the New Jersey railway, for my desired and happy home.

I was met at Wall Street Wharf, Philadelphia, by a large party of friends and the Frankfort brass band, mounted on a new omnibus called the "Wallett," with a fine portrait of myself on the door, and one in the character of jester on each side of the vehicle. So we went out in grand procession to Frankfort, where I was heartily welcomed by my friends and neighbours. My enjoyment of home, however, was transient, for I soon had to bury my dear little American daughter in the Laurel Hill Cemetery, near to the house in which she had been a ray of sunshine.

I shortly afterwards left Frankfort for a tour with Ballard and Bailey again, travelling through Pennsylvania, up to Indianapolis, through Indiana, and so on through the Green River country. We performed a day at Bowling Green *en route*, little dreaming that such a peaceful and luxuriant country would, a few years afterwards, be dyed with the blood of many of her noblest sons. Through the severe sickness of the proprietors, who suffered from a disorder known as "whiskey fever," they were unable to attend properly to their business, which went rapidly to ruin. They were indebted to me about six hundred dollars; so I pretended (?) to get drunk, and kicked up a jolly row with the manager. In the heat of his passion he paid me all my money, and discharged me instanter. I felt very grateful for this, especially on hearing, next day, that Madame Tournaire, the principal equestrienne, to whom they owed some three thousand dollars, found it impossible to get from them six dollars to buy boots. So I went on my way rejoicing, and made for Memphis, Tennessee, where, with some difficulty, I converted my dollars into gold. At least, I obtained gold for four hundred; for many of the notes I held were of banks that had either broken or had never existed.

Here I was fortunate enough to drop on Spaulding and Rogers again. Their company was visiting the river towns, carrying the tent, horses, &c., on a steamboat, commanded by Captain Sparhawk. I made arrangements to travel with them up the Mississippi to Vicksburg, Natchez-under-the-hill, up the Ohio, visiting the towns on the Kentucky side on the upward voyage, calling at Louisville, and up as high as Pitsburg, running to Cincinnati, and down to Cairo at the mouth of the river again. We then visited all the Mississippi towns as high as St. Louis, and then took a trip on the Upper Mississippi to Galena, Iowa, coming from that state to towns in Illinois, Quincy, &c. We also performed at Nauvoo of the Mormons, where I boarded at the house of the widow of their late prophet, Joe Smith. We then passed up the rapids, and travelled as high as the Falls of St. Paul.

Our mode of operations was as follows : On mooring to the banks of a river adjacent to a town, a large marquee, brackets, and seats, were carried ashore, and fitted up contiguous to the river. This constituted our circus.

In this expedition I again had the pleasure of meeting my old friend Jack the Giant Killer, but, fortunately, I was not an actor in that world-renowned legendary drama. The giants and giantesses greatly astonished the slave population, who testified their admiration by unearthly yells and horrible grimaces. They threw themselves into the most frantic attitudes ; occasionally falling backwards, and tumbling through the seats in the exuberance of their childish enjoyment. We had a favourite trick we played upon the negroes at the conclusion of our performances, which was generally about dusk hour. As soon as the audience had left the large tent, John Murray, a gentleman who played the banjo extremely well, would sing and play in the dressing-room, until a crowd of negroes, who are passionately fond of music, would assemble outside to listen. When they had been thus engaged for some time, a party of us would take some short stakes and a long rope, and going near the gate of the field, would drive down the stakes in a line at short distances, and then tie the rope to the stakes six or eight inches from the ground, the banjo engrossing their attention all the time. As soon as the signal was given that all was prepared, three of the performers were enclosed in the enormous framework of the giants. In an instant the side of the canvas would be raised; when giants and giantesses, clubs in hand, rushed out among the affrighted darkies, who fled away with fleet feet, making the nearest way to the gate. They often amounted to two or three hundred. In the hasty retreat and dim light, not observing the low rope, the front rank would be tripped up, and the others rolling over them, would pile up a hecatomb of black humanity. Then the stuffed clubs of the giants made awful havoc amongst them, and the terrified mob cried out "Murder," and implored mercy. The greater number tremblingly believing the giants were realities.

Other experiments we used to make at the expense of the darkies. In sailing on the Mississippi, we often ran so close to the banks as to be able to speak to the slaves working on the plantations. We frequently enlivened their labours by the band playing on the hurricane deck. It was a treat to see the poor fellows rush to the side, and nearly run themselves out of breath to keep up with the steamer, their ears drinking in the sweet sounds of our music. Sometimes, when we knew we were approaching a plantation where a large number of negroes were employed, we fired guns, rang the great bell of the boat, blew the steam-whistle, beat gongs, and raised a terrible din to attract attention as to a ship in distress. Then, when we arrived nearly abreast of the crowd we had congregated, we would bring out the double-headed giant and the single-headed giant, and the giantess, who would pursue the performers and crew with their clubs. As we had several children on board, belonging to Madigan and Carroll, the giantess would amuse herself by swallowing one after another of them. Guns were fired at the giants, and desperate resistance made. This performance would create a terrible panic amongst the spectators on shore, who verily believed the whole of the passengers and crew were about to be murdered and devoured by monstrous and cannibal pirates. Before they could ascertain our fate, the rapid steamer bore us out of their sight.

CHAPTER VII.

"Now my task is smoothly done,
I can fly or I can run
Quickly to the green earth's end."—*Comus.*

AS I had now been several years from England, I resolved to return to my native land. I took a cabin passage on board the good ship City of Glasgow, Captain Wylie. After a favourable voyage, I reached Liverpool in safety.

My first business was very pleasant. The prosperity I had enjoyed in my travels enabled me to pay into the Insolvent Court of Leeds the whole amount of my indebtedness when I left England. On the proposal of Mr. Harle, who was formerly the solicitor for my only opposing creditor, Mr. Batty, his honour the judge, — Marshall, Esq., directed that, in consideration of my honourable conduct, the expenses of the court should be paid out of the estate. His honour, in open court, expressed his approbation of my upright dealing. and his regret that he had not oftener such an opportunity of commendation. This I felt to be a satisfactory recompence for the perils I had undergone from stormy voyages, yellow fever, cholera, boiler explosions, and railway accidents. I had cleared my character, and felt like the "Village Blacksmith," who

> "Looks the whole world in the face,
> For he owes not any man."

I was further rewarded by the presentation of a massive gold cup, bearing the following inscription—

"Presented to W. F. Wallett, Esq., the jester, as a mark of esteem from his friends. Committee—David Orange, William Pegg, James Nall, Robert Burnham.

"Lion and Lamb Hotel, Leicester, March, 1859."

Previous to leaving the United States I arranged with Pablo Fanque to meet me at Liverpool, that I should make my first appearance at the Amphitheatre, and that he should take me on a starring tour with his company through Yorkshire and Lancashire, where I was sure of a good reception after so long an absence. I had brought with me a splendid American carriage, harness, bills and lithographs of mammoth size. To my surprise Mr. Pablo did not appear, and for days I could not find any one who had the least idea where he was. At length I found letters from him at the post office, dated from Paisley, stating his inability to carry out the engagement, but expressing a wish to meet me, and see what could be done. I went over, and found that he had been playing a season at the Theatre Royal, Glasgow, with James Cooke in the large circus on the green, in opposition to him. In this contest Pablo had come off second best, and retired to Paisley. We soon came to an arrangement, and immediately began to erect in Glasgow the first circular amphitheatre ever built in Scotland. I played with him in Paisley for two weeks, and then with his consent took an engagement at Franconi's Cirque in the city of Dublin. The business was enormous; for on my return to Paisley, after paying all expenses, my share of the fortnight's receipts amounted to £200. All this time our new building in Glasgow was progressing, and we opened it at the fair time. It was now Pablo's turn to crow over his rival, for after remaining a month with fearful business, Cooke left my friend in undisputed possession of the field. The season was a succession of triumphs. One of the principal attractions was a little Irishman whom I engaged in Dublin, who rejoiced in the name of Vilderini, one of the best posture masters the theatrical world ever produced. I engaged him for three months at a liberal salary, on the express understanding that I should shave his head, and convert him into a Chinaman. For which nationality his small eyes, pug nose, high cheek bones, and heavy mouth admirably adapted him. So his head was shaved, all but a small tuft on the top, to which a saddler with waxed twine firmly attached his celestial pig-tail. His eyebrows were shaved off, and his face, neck, and head dyed after the most admired Chinese complexion. Thus metamorphosed, he was announced on the walls as :—

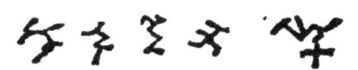

KI HI CHIN FAN FOO
Man-Spider-leg mortal.

We had about twenty supernumeraries and the whole equestrian company in Chinese costume. Variegated lanterns, gongs, drums, and cymbals ushered the distinguished Chinaman into the ring, to give his wonderful entertainment. The effect was astonishing, and its success extraordinary. In fact the entire get-up was so well carried out that it occasioned us some annoyance. For there were two rival tea merchants in Glasgow at the time, and each of them had engaged a genuine Chinaman as touter at his door. Every night, as soon as they could escape from their groceries, they came to the circus to solicit an interview with their compatriot. After being denied many nights in succession, they peremptorily demanded to see him. Being again refused, they determined to move for the writ of *habeas corpus*. That is to say, they applied to the magistrate stating they believed their countryman to be deprived of his liberty except during the time of his performance. We were then compelled to produce our celestial actor, who proved to the satisfaction of the worthy magistrate that he was a free Irishman from Tipperary.

After an unexampled run at Glasgow, I bade adieu to my friend and partner, and the thriving city, repeating with heart and voice its own motto, "Let Glasgow flourish." After various engagements with provincial equestrian companies, I joined Mr. John Tonks, Hernandez, Stone, and Newsome at Bingley Hall, Birmingham. During this season I was presented by the townspeople and the esteemed director, John Tonks, Esq., with a massive silver candelabra and épergne, bearing the following inscription :—

"Presented to W. F. Wallett at Tonks's Coliseum, Bingley Hall, Birmingham, March 3rd, 1854, by Mr. Campbell, on behalf of a number of friends, who admiring his public talent and private worth, have thus ventured to express their regard."

It was publicly presented to me by Mr. Andrew Campbell, who made a very happy speech on the occasion. He is now an inmate of the Theatrical College, where I trust his declining days will be spent in peace and comfort. From Birmingham I went to Kidderminster, and took the management for Mr. Pablo. At Worcester I obtained possession of the splendid hall, and fitted it up as an elegant circus. I formed a magnificent ring. The horses ran on a cocoa-nut pile matting, the centre of the arena being covered with Brussels carpet, thereby avoiding the dust and dirt of the ordinary sawdust floor. The patronage bestowed upon us was unequalled in the history of Worcester; but notwithstanding the favour of the public, my ill luck again overtook me. For Batty came down, holding a bill of sale from Mr. Pablo, and in the most wanton and unfeeling manner sold up the whole concern. This ruined my friend Pablo, upset my arrangements, and for a time blighted my prospects.

My next speculation was to arrange with Mr. Copeland of the Amphitheatre, Liverpool, to provide him with a company, horses, wardrobe, property, &c., at so much a week for two months, commencing on Boxing night. Now the whole property at Worcester had been sold in one lot, and bought by Batty, who arranged with Pablo to manage it as before. Hearing this, and knowing that Pablo had no building ready, I wrote to him offering terms for him to join me at Liverpool, which he accepted. This saved me much trouble, for I had only to reinforce the troupe to be ready for action. So I engaged several first-class artists, Richard Hemming, William O'Dale, and others, male and female. So far so good. Everything ready, and my mind at perfect ease. So I invited a few friends to dine with me on Christmas Day. In the midst of our festivity, however, I received a letter from Pablo stating that Batty would not allow him to fulfil his engagement with me. This was a most serious matter; for the performance was to commence next night, and I had not a single horse or the command of one. Still worse, I had engaged eight horse boxes and carriage trucks, which were collected at Worcester, ready to run the company to Liverpool at any moment. The evil genius of Batty marred everything. He has long gone to his last account, and I hope enjoys that happiness he suffered none to experience below who had the misfortune to come under his power. However, sitting down by the road side to cry is no way to get the cart out of the mud. Shoulder to wheel, and on you go. Old Jack Clarke was at this time erecting a dukey in the park, for the gratification of the juvenile Dicky Sams during the holidays. So jumping up from the festive board and doffing my holiday garments, I prepared myself for hard work and a long journey. The first move was to find Clarke, who had three horses. I soon settled with him, and had his horses removed to my stables. I also engaged his three clever boys. So with O'Dale, Hemming, and the others, I had formed the nucleus of the troupe. After giving proper instructions to my agent, I left Liverpool by the night mail train, and arrived in London at four next morning. At five I was at Mr. William Cooke's bedroom door, at Astley's Theatre, where I soon engaged eight ring horses, a menage horse, and Thomas Cooke and his pony Prince, with his son James as rider, and himself to act as ringmaster.

Performers, horses, and wardrobe were hastily collected at Euston Square station at ten o'clock. We arrived at Liverpool in time to appear and give great satisfaction to a crowded and enthusiastic audience. The season was a paying one, and on the last night I received from Mr.

Copeland a very high compliment. He came to my room with two bottles of champagne, we drank each other's healths, and I expressed my thanks for his urbanity and kindness during our engagement. He expressed his satisfaction at the manner in which I had catered for the public, and concluded by saying, "I have been many years manager, Mr. Wallett. I have had many gentlemen join me, but you are the only one that ever left me as such."

I next joined Madame Macarte at Carlisle for six nights. We opened to a crowded house. Business continued good up to Friday, my benefit night. I had a settlement with the manageress every night, on the principle of no song no supper. By this time I had become thoroughly homesick, and having left my family in America, and being unwell, felt very anxious to return there. Friday night I sat alone in my hotel, taking my unshared meal in very low spirits, when the waiter handed me a letter from Bill O'Dale, whom I had left in Liverpool. He informed me of his intention to return home in the steamship Baltic on the morrow, Saturday, and wished me to see him off. This gave me my cue. My mind was instantly made up. I paid my hotel bill, packed my luggage, had it removed to the railway station, attended to my duties, and received my share of the benefit. I left the railway station at 12 o'clock and arrived at Liverpool at 5 a.m. My things were sent on board the Baltic. I took a passage ticket, unknown to any of my friends, and merely appeared to go with a party on the tug boat to see our friend O'Dale off. The tug was fully an hour alongside the packet, so there was ample time for leave-taking and a parting glass. When the second bell of the tug was rung as a signal for all the shore folks to leave the packet, I hid myself in the steward's pantry. Then as soon as I heard the gun fire, and the vessel move a-head, and the three hearty cheers that rose from the leave-takers, I rushed on deck, jumped on the bulwarks, and in the most frantic manner shouted for the vessel to stop. But I knew it was more than the captain's berth was worth to stop when the vessel was once under way. So I was apparently carried off against my will. I acquainted the purser with the facts of the case, and he agreed to keep up the deception during the whole of the voyage. Not even my friend O'Dale suspected the truth for some days.

After a tempestuous voyage we arrived at New York all well. Once ashore I was soon down at Florence's Hotel, and found a host of old friends there. The moment I entered my arrival was telegraphed all over the house. "Here's Wallett come. Come here, old fellow, what'll you have to drink?" "Oh, a little cold brandy and water," said I. "No, I'll be hanged if you do," said half a dozen voices at once. "Here, Lockwood, bring us a basket of Schreider's champagne." Oh, what a hearty welcome! How different to my reception at Liverpool, after an absence of seven years from my native land, that boasts so much of its hospitality! As soon as I landed there, I went to a house where I had spent many a score of pounds, and been the cause of hundreds being expended there. On my entrance the following conversation took place: "Good day, sir." "Is this Mr. Wallett? Bless me, what a time it is since I saw you. Where have you been this long time?" "Oh, I've been to the United States." "Oh, indeed; and how did you like America and the Yankees?" "First rate." "And how's Mrs. Wallett; and are you very well; and when did you arrive?" After answering a score of such questions, which considerably added to my thirst, I said, "Give me a little cold brandy and water." "Four or six, sir?" said he. With ill-concealed disgust I said, "Six; will you take one yourself?" He didn't mind if he did. So I expended a shilling in good old English hospitality, the liquor being measured in a thing about the size of a thimble.

I arrived safely at home, and played a brief engagement at the National Circus, Philadelphia, with Mr. Rufus Welch. I was, however, not allowed much time to rest at home. For Mr. Frank Rivers had just arrived from California, to engage a company to go there and join Rowe and Smith. Through the inducement of a great salary I consented to undertake the journey. At the end of my engagement with Mr. Welch, he kindly gave me a free benefit, as a farewell previous to my departure for the land of gold. Out of gratitude I record the fact that all the equestrians, vaulters, acrobats, &c., in both New York and Philadelphia volunteered their gratuitous services. I had upwards of sixty artistes appearing at the same time in the ring, forming two troupes of vaulters, one headed by Mose Lipman and the other by O'Dale. It was on that very night, after the performance, that our highly respected and much lamented manager and friend, Rufus Welch, departed this life. All who knew him will say "He was a man, that, take him for all in all, we ne'er shall look upon his like again."

CHAPTER VIII.

"Of moving accidents by flood and field,
Of hair-breadth 'scapes."—*Othello*.

WE embarked at New York in the steam ship Illinois, on her voyage to Aspinwall. We had at least fifteen hundred passengers. Just before the time of starting a telegram arrived from Washington to detain the ship, to take on board three companies of United States' infantry, with their officers and baggage. It was a bitter cold day, and hundreds upon hundreds of anxious faces thronged the wharves to bid perhaps a last adieu to those near and dear to them. The detention of the ship only seemed to prolong the sorrow of parting. Just at that time Henry Russell's great song of "Cheer, boys, cheer," was very popular. When the soldiers at last marched on board, the bell was rung, the ropes cast off, and the signal gun fired. Then I mounted the paddle box, and with all the energy I could muster commenced the chorus of "Cheer, boys, cheer." This was instantly taken up with one accord by hundreds that crowded the decks, and thousands that thronged the wharves. Eyes seemed to brighten through their tears, sad faces wore a smile, heavy hearts were lightened, and it appeared as if this little simple song had revived the dying hopes of the vast multitude. It was wafted from the ship, and echoed from the shore, until the sound of the cheerful voices was lost in the distance.

It was pretty throng work on board I assure you. There were so many to be provided for, that there were three separate breakfasts, dinners, and teas, filling the immense saloon nearly all day long. We had a very boisterous voyage, and nearly foundered in a terrible storm off Cape Hatteras, which is as famous for its hurricanes as Manchester for its rain. However, after considerable buffeting we made a first rate run through the Gulf of Mexico and the Caribbean Sea, and arrived all well at Aspinwall, or Navy Bay. We crossed the isthmus of Panama by the new railway. I had very agreeable companions, Burnell Runnells, Tom King, Billy Larue, Frank Whitaker, Frank Rivers, Mrs. Whitaker, and others. Rather dear railway travelling in this part of the world. The distance is little more than from Manchester to Liverpool, and the second class fare is five pounds. Forty pounds of luggage allowed free, and twelve and a half cents or sixpence per pound charged for excess. I made a rough calculation during our trip, and found that with the immense amount of mails, parcels, passengers, and general freight, the traffic between the two oceans must on that day have realized about thirty thousand dollars.

We had several hours to spare on arriving at what is called Panama, where the railway depôt and the shipping wharf on the Pacific are situated. This place is entirely new, having been erected for the accommodation of the traffic, and nearly all the buildings are hotels, refreshment rooms, money changers', gold buyers', and outfitting establishments. The ancient city of Panama is at a considerable distance, more in the hollow of the bay. We took a trip to see this old city, which is very fine indeed, with some noble buildings, both public and private, the principal of which is a grand old cathedral. After seeing all that was considered worthy of note, we returned to the quay, just in time to gain a seat in the last boat. For we had to be conveyed about two miles to the steamship the John L. Stephens, which was riding under the shelter of a lofty island in the bay. The steamer was of colossal size and had three decks; the upper or hurricane deck was level with the top of the paddle-boxes, and of the entire width of the ship. So, with the interruption only of the masts and funnel, there was a clear promenade three hundred feet long by seventy feet wide. This was surmounted by a milk-white awning, supported on iron stanchions. Strange to say, this immense ship had only one engine, but certainly the largest cylinder, and the longest stroke I ever saw.

On the third day of the voyage—Oh, what a lovely morning! It was Sunday. The sky was cloudless, and the sun shining in glorious refulgence was reflected in the blue waters of the Pacific Ocean, which was as bright and clear as a polished mirror. Peace reigned supreme, as if all nature acknowledged it was the Sabbath of the Lord. Not a sound was heard, except the low groaning of the steam giant in the bowels of our ship, and the dashing of his powerful arms as he churned the pure water into silvery foam. Who could imagine that the angel of death was hovering over the tranquil and lovely sea! A loud cry was heard, "Man overboard!" and in a moment all was bustle and confusion. Ladies and children rushed upon deck, and many tears bedewed their cheeks as they watched the poor fellow being left further and further astern. We could see him holding up his hands at intervals, as if imploring our help. The captain roared out, " Stop her! Starboard your helm!" The good ship came round like a thing of life. The boat was rapidly lowered and eagerly manned. They pushed from the ship, and pulled away with agony of apprehension lest they should be too late. Many were the prayers offered up for the salvation of the life in peril, and many hearts beat for the poor soul that they had never known. The boat nears him—he is still afloat—they gain the spot—the boatswain reaches for him—but, alas, he has sunk! In a moment a sailor dives from the boat to rescue him, but in vain. Again he dives, and again coming to the surface, is so exhausted that it is with difficulty he is recovered. For a few moments they watch with breathless anxiety. Alas! the poor fellow is gone, gone for ever! The boat's crew return dejectedly to the ship; the boat is hoisted to the davits; the captain calls out " Go ahead!" and to the helmsman, " Keep your course!" and the ship is once more on her voyage. The sailors descend to the forecastle. They are sad and silent, and the empty hammock and vacated chest will long remind them of their lost shipmate.

It becoming known that the poor sailor had left a wife and five children in Liverpool, nearly all on board contributed to their succour; their donations amounting to a considerable sum. The captain kindly gave me the use of the great saloon, and I delivered two lectures for the same object, realizing about two hundred and twenty dollars.

During a great portion of the voyage, our course was within sight of the high mountains of Mexico. The cliffs are very imposing. Near the sea there are hundreds of miles of almost perpendicular rocks, which assume all kinds of fantastic shapes; here resembling enormous castles, batteries, and bastions, and there more like colossal cathedrals with tall spires, pinnacles, and minarets. The background of pale blue mountains, rising eight or ten thousand feet high, gave the scene an enchanting effect.

While sailing along this beautiful coast, the vessel's course was suddenly altered from nearly due west to north, going at full speed. It appeared as if in a few minutes she must be dashed against the rocks, which were now soaring thousands of feet above our heads. In a moment however we discovered a small opening, a mere rent in the cliff. It was very narrow, but I was informed the channel was immensely deep. We ran through this strait for some distance, and then altering our course again to westward we suddenly found ourselves in the finest sheltered harbour in the world, the Bay of Acapulco, which is nearly surrounded by inaccessible mountains. This bay is the shelter for fishermen who hunt the spermaceti whale. Here we took in water and several bullocks, the largest of which was nearly the size of a donkey, and almost all horns and tail. As we were densely crowded in the ship, and the weather was very hot, the doctor advised the captain to let none go ashore, and not to permit fruit vendors to come on board. But such orders are more easily given than enforced. In less than a quarter of an hour there were scores of boats around us laden with different kinds of fruit. People on deck were pulling fruit up by strings attached to caps, pitching their money into the boats. People in the boats were tying fruit up in handkerchiefs, and throwing it on board and into the cabin windows and port holes. Our vessel was built on purpose for the station, and her saloon-deck, from stem to stern, was pierced with large port holes, with regular house windows to them, about six feet square. So the boatmen drove a roaring trade. We remained at anchor a few hours, and then the good ship gallantly steamed out of the narrow entrance once more on her way to the Gulf of California.

I must here state that the John L. Stephens was the best regulated ship I ever sailed in. All the first class able-bodied passengers were trained every day by the captain and officers, and divided into small military companies and a fire brigade. There were four fire engines on the quarter deck, and two powerful pumps amidship, worked by the engine of the vessel. It was our duty at the roll of the drum by day or night to hasten on deck to our allotted stations. An officer and six men, with loaded rifles, were placed in charge of each boat, which the sailors packed with a barrel of biscuit, a barrel of water, compass, &c. They then swung the boats off by the davits, and stood fall in hand, ready to lower away. It was the duty of each party to guard the boats from being seized by the steerage passengers, and to keep them at any risk for the women and children. The duty of the fire brigade was to screw on the hose and nozzles, and throw up jets of water everywhere. In fact so perfectly were we trained, that in less than three minutes from the first roll of the drum I have seen six powerful streams of water thrown as high as the mast head, and the boats provisioned and manned ready to leave the vessel as if for ever. To prevent alarm, the ladies were always acquainted by the stewardess when it was intended to have a night drill. They were so grateful to us for our devotion that they worked us a pair of colours, which were presented to us on the quarter-deck by the fair hands of Mrs. Marshall North, with a very complimentary speech, supplemented by thanks and half a dozen baskets of champagne from our worthy Commander, Captain Pearson.

After a long but pleasant voyage we steamed up Vermillion Bay, and moored at the wharf at San Francisco. There were several thousands to welcome us. For as steam boats arrived only once a fortnight, all business was suspended, and a general holiday commenced as soon as the vessel was signalled in sight, although it was known she would take several hours to arrive. As soon as we came within speaking distance, we were greeted with cheers from the assembled crowd, which we returned in good earnest from our ship. Then followed a confusion of tongues worthy of Babel. "Holloa Joe, holloa Jem, —Jack—Brown! How are you? Is our Dick on board? Are my wife and children there?" Others, who expected none of their kin, contented themselves with the news they could glean from our latest newspapers. It is a common practice with the New York and Boston papers, especially with the police gazettes, for the copies destined for remote parts to be dated about the time the packet is expected to arrive. By this means the paper loses its apparent antiquity. I had carefully saved all my papers, of which I had one or two hundred, now in great demand.

Many thanks to Horace Greeley, Gordon Bennett, Colonel Wallace, friend Church, and others, I was abundantly supplied with Tribunes, Heralds, Philadelphia Suns, Ledgers, and Pennsylvanians. Knowing their value on landing—though I lent them during the voyage—I carefully collected them in again, and was thus enabled to give a great treat to the Californians. I got up quite an excitement by bringing up bundles of papers on the paddle boxes, and scrambling them among the eager mob. One gentleman, who stood aloof, said to me afterwards, "Have you another paper to spare?" "Yes, would you like this morning's paper?" He did not appear well pleased, thinking I was chaffing him. But I had one of the post-dated Boston papers, and it happened curiously enough it was dated the very day of our arrival. I assured him I was not joking, and offered again to give him the paper. He looked like St. Thomas, and said, "If you do, I will stand a bottle of champagne." I soon produced the paper, which raised a hearty laugh among the bystanders at my sold friend, in which he goodnaturedly joined. We went to the International Hotel to discuss the champagne, and thus I had the good fortune to gain a sincere friend. Our mutual good feeling was never impaired during my stay in the country, and I yet live in the hope of renewing our intercourse.

The same evening, while strolling down to Tom Maguire's Opera House, I met one of our female passengers, a little English woman who had come from Leeds to join her husband at the gold diggings. She had no friend to protect her during the long journey, but the heavy charge on her hands of a child seven years of age.

Her husband was to have met her at the wharf, but had disappointed her. She had seen many happy reunions that day of husbands and wives long separated, hugged in each other's embrace, unable to speak except with tears of joy. This poor lonely woman, with her little boy in hand, was almost broken-hearted when I met her. I gave her some lemonade; the boy wished for an apple. I got him a very fine one, for I knew he would enjoy it after the voyage. I put six more in the corner of her shawl, saying they would do for her little boy another time. She returned the apples, saying that perhaps in that climate they might disagree with him. Lucky for me, for on asking the price of the apples I found that they were only a dollar each!

We found every thing prepared for our reception and the opening of the season. The circus was erected on a piece of waste ground next to the International Hotel. This was a first class establishment, and considering the country the prices were very moderate. It was here I first met the eminent tragedian, Kean Buchanan. One day at dinner the waiter inquired what he would take. Before replying, he turned to his secretary, and asked, "What do I act to-night?" The reply was "Hamlet." He then said to the waiter in a subdued tone, "Give me a little boiled chicken well done." I suppose if he had been about to perform Richard III. he would have ordered roast beef underdone, as more appropriate to the part. Buchanan took a tour through the northern and southern mines with the theatrical company, at the same time that I went with Rowe and Smith's Great Circus. Just before this time the legislature had passed a bill to put down cock-fighting, bull-fighting, and bear-baiting on Sunday. It was called an "Act for the prohibition of noisy and barbarous entertainments on the Sabbath." We had arrived on our route at the city of Coloma. It was just at the end of this town, where gold was first discovered in California. It was washed up in the mill race belonging to old General Suter. The mill had fallen into disuse and decay. I brought a piece of the wood-work away and have it now. I also cut a walking stick from the manzineta tree which grew within ten yards of the spot where the gold was found. Well, on Sunday Kean Buchanan was to have opened for a week on the same day as ourselves for one night; but knowing that we should be the great attraction for that day, he deferred his opening till our departure. This drew upon him a stinging criticism. Next morning's paper remarked, "Rowe and Smith's Circus paid us a visit yesterday, and was densely crowded both performances. The theatre was to have opened, but did not. Kean Buchanan was to have acted Hamlet, which was thus postponed. Perhaps he was afraid his acting of the part would come under the new law that prohibits noisy and barbarous entertainments on the Sabbath."

With Rowe's company I had the pleasure of visiting not only the city, but the whole splendid valley of the Sacramento, Marysville, Stockton, Nevada, and all the towns in the northern and southern mines. While in the latter, I was favoured with an invitation to dine at a certain hotel. When I arrived there, I was surprised on finding it was kept by Mrs. Briggs, formerly the landlady of the beerhouse opposite Astley's stage door. She had provided for me a fine leg of mutton, Yorkshire pudding, and all the proper accessaries to an English dinner.

We went as high as Mud Springs, Diamond Springs, Horsefall Bend, Yankee Jems, and other euphonious places. At Nevada, Burnell Runnells and I had a narrow escape from death. One night after the conclusion of the performance, we strolled out and looked in at a large saloon. This was divided into three departments. In one was a fandango party, comprised of Chilian, Mexican, and Spanish women, with a motley crew of men of all colours, languages, and nationalities. The second was devoted to refreshment, drinking, and card playing. The third to a game called "kino." There were ten or fifteen miners round the table, on which were piled immense quantities of gold for which they were playing. Some desperate ruffians entered, and I immediately suspected mischief. Burnell and I were unfortunately unarmed. The place was brilliantly illuminated with camphine lamps. At the report of a pistol every lamp was instantly extinguished. I darted under the table like a shot, and pulled Burnell by the leg down beside me. Never shall I forget the horror of this moment. I could hear the heavy thud of bludgeons, and knew knives were doing their deadly work. Hot life's blood streamed towards where we lay. The whole affair lasted about a minute or two, though it seemed an age to us. At length lights were brought in, and the rekindled lamps revealed the scene of an awful tragedy. Scarcely a vestige of the gold remained, and the miners we had just seen in lusty enjoyment, lay around butchered and mangled in the most terrible manner. We speedily made our exit from this chamber of horrors, and made tracks for our hotel.

This building was constructed of framework, the walls

and roof being formed of unbleached calico. The doors were covered with black muslin, to distinguish them from the walls. The partitions of the rooms were so thin, and the beds so small, that if you turned over incautiously in the night, your knees were very likely to interrupt the slumber of some gentleman in the next apartment.

After our experience at the gambling room, we resolved never to travel or go out at night without being well armed. This was a wise resolution; for my repeating rifle saved my life. I forgot to tell you that during our voyage poor Burnell had some complaint of the eyes. We were at one time fearful he would lose his sight altogether. When his eyes began to mend, he was ordered by the doctor to bathe them several times a day in weak brandy and water. On board ship he could not obtain less than a bottle at a time, so there was generally a good stock of eye-water. Now I had given up my lower berth to my invalid friend, who kept his brandy bottle at one corner of the pillow. As there was an opening between my bunk and the ship's side, I could slip my hand down when Burnell was asleep, and refresh myself from his bottle of lotion. It was really astonishing to him how his eyes could have drunk so much brandy; but he had not pledged me in the words of the old song, "Drink to me only with thine eyes." I was bowled out at last though, for one night, thinking he was asleep, I reached down for a sweet stolen draught, and he, at the same time, wishing to pour a little brandy into his saucer, our hands met on the bottle. "Oh, that's it, is it?" He resolved to take the value of the brandy out of me, as soon as daylight enabled him to see me as an antagonist. But, happily, the settlement was postponed, and he now took his revenge in the following manner. We were walking on the road in front of our caravans, in the vicinity of Volcano. I had left the road, and wandered alone into a chaperelle of the manzineta tree, like the arched cloisters of a cathedral. Suddenly I found myself precipitated into a chasm some twelve or fifteen feet deep. It was a hunting pit belonging to some trapper in the neighbourhood, and had been beautifully prepared, for I never noticed any difference between the top of the trap and the surrounding ground. It was, no doubt, designed for the accommodation of a grisly bear or cayotte. Having fallen on the soft stuff I carried down with me, I was unhurt, except by bewilderment. Recovering from the shock of the crash of the breaking branches and the report of my rifle, which exploded as I fell, I soon felt anxiety regarding my fate. Burnell, who was walking quietly along the road, and had never missed me, heard my gun fire, and, thinking I had come across some game, returned to my assistance. Luckily, I had a good stock of ammunition; for it was not till after I had fired four or five rounds that I could attract his attention to where I was buried; and there was not the slightest chance of my getting out without assistance. At last he found me. Then came his hour of revenge. Lying on the ground, and looking down into the trap, he said, "Now I've got you; now I'll make you pay for the brandy you robbed my poor eyes of." I begged, and threatened, and swore by turns, without avail. He would not relieve me, and it appeared at one time as if he would have left me to my fate. It might have been days before the trapper came round and discovered the strange and, perhaps, starved animal he had caught. So I was compelled solemnly to promise to pay for a bottle of the best brandy. At this time the wheels of our waggons and the tramp of the horses could be heard in the distance. Burnell fired a gun to attract attention, and with the aid of one of the tent guy ropes and two tent men, I was hauled to the surface of the earth.

While in California, I visited the giant trees at Murphy's Camp, Calaveras County. I had the pleasure of viewing the Wellingtonia Gigantea, the Washingtonia Gigantea, and three splendid specimens that grow together, and are called "The Three Graces." Their average height I was informed, was estimated at four hundred and fifty feet, and their diameter, twenty feet from the ground, clear of the root branches, was upwards of thirty-six feet. I took photographs of them, but was unfortunately robbed of these in Sacramento. The bark of the Wellingtonia Gigantea had been removed, and was afterwards an object of great interest in the Crystal Palace, Sydenham, until it was destroyed in the fire of 1866. The largest of all is one that has fallen down, and is in a state of decay. I rode on a four-horse omnibus, with twenty other passengers, inside of the bark, resembling a railway tunnel, for a length of one hundred and seventy feet.

Another curious feature in California is the Chinese element of the population. They have entire quarters to themselves in the different cities, and separate camps at the mines, where every thing is as peculiarly Chinese as the design of the willow plates. They have their theatres, which are entirely devoid of scenery, machinery, and the usual apparatus of the modern drama. In a battle scene, where a dozen of them have been put *hors de combat*, the dead and wounded would rise up and walk after a miraculous manner. There is a continual din kept up by twelve or fourteen musicians who sit at the back of the stage, all in a row, like the tailors in the old song. On one occasion when I visited the theatre, there was an usurping prince who wished to oust his rightful sovereign from the throne. In the heat of passion, he struck the queen a blow which felled her to the ground. This, as it soon appeared, produced premature labour. To my horror, the dear baby was taken from the fallen queen, and proclaimed the lawful heir to the celestial crown, thus frustrating the knavish tricks of the usurper. The performances were carried on day and night, without intermission, by relays of actors, the audience arriving and departing at pleasure. Very often I have seen a man prepare his little opium pipe, and smoke himself into sweet oblivion. Then some friend would roll him from his seat, and pack him underneath, there to slumber in peace till the return of consciousness

Many of the productions of the Chinese are truly wonderful. I purchased of one an ivory ball two inches in diameter, in which were six other balls that could be removed by a pin, all carved out of the same piece. Also an ivory balance or steel-yard used by their doctors, that would weigh accurately as little as a third of a grain. As a proof of their economy, I knew a tailor who cooked his dinner by his goose. He had an utensil that appeared like a saucepan, but on examination, I found it was a highly polished iron vessel holding burning charcoal. On this was a cooking pot vessel holding lama beans. When he wanted to press a garment he removed his dinner for a moment, and ironed the vestment to perfect smoothness with the polished bottom of the stove.

While in this country I bought an interest in a travelling show, and having two partners upon whose honesty I could not depend, I endeavoured to find a trustworthy gentleman to act as treasurer. One was recommended to me as a young man of honesty and perseverance, who had been ruined by a fire which consumed his whole stock-in-trade, which was uninsured. I am happy to record his conduct justified the character I received of him. On my departure from San Francisco, he desired to have my portrait, and I of course requested his. While sitting he said, "Will you wait for another of mine? It is seven long years since I saw my dear mother, and I should like you to take her my likeness, as you are returning to Philadelphia, my native home."

It was hard parting with so many friends as I had made here. Scores came to bid me a kind adieu. A committee presented me with a gold watch and chain, which I now wear, and a magnificent Canton crape shawl; and Rochet, a clown, made me a present of a solid gold ornament in the shape of a horse, with appendage. The gun fired, the hawsers were cast adrift, and the noble ship Golden Gate steamed away from the shore, where a hundred loving hearts invoked as many blessings on my departing head.

Soon after arriving at home, I visited the mother of my Californian friend. I found her among the upper-ten-dom of Philadelphia, near Twelfth and Walnut Street, and, to my surprise, she was a Quakeress. The production of her son's portrait procured me a warm welcome, and after shedding tears of joy over the image of her boy, she said,

"And how long is it since thou hast seen my lad?" I replied, "Within two months." She exclaimed, "Let me gaze upon the eyes that have looked on him." I returned home after many exchanges of good wishes, with a pressing invitation to pay her another visit. I shortly afterwards did so. I found her with a large party of Friends, and had a very enjoyable evening, during which I described my journeys in California, &c. On my retiring, the old lady (for obvious reasons I omit her name) invited me into a private room, and said, "We shall always welcome thee as a friend, but in my anxiety to hear about my son, I forgot to ask thee thy name or trade. What art thou?" I told her I was the clown at the National Circus. She exclaimed, "Oh, dear! I've always been taught to imagine that men in thy profession were devils, but after what I've seen and heard, if ever thou appears in Philadelphia, I shall come and see thee." In the course of a few weeks I did appear, and shortly afterwards received an invitation from the mother of my friend. After a kind reception, she said, "Well, I have been to hear thee and to see thee. Thou knowest I could not go in this garb, so I borrowed a shawl and bonnet of Mary our maid, and went to thy circus. Thou art not a clown, thou art not a buffoon; thou art a high moral teacher, and I regret the ignorance that has led me to condemn thy class for so many years." The great cause of the animosity between different classes is to be traced to a want of a proper knowledge of each other's feelings and motives.

CHAPTER IX.

"And frame my face to all occasions."—King Henry VI.

AFTER a short tour in the Northern States, I once more returned to England. I visited my native town, and renewed many old and pleasant acquaintances, and then determined to make a tour in the provinces. As several of the circus proprietors had combined and resolved not to give me my terms, I made up my mind to engage a tight-rope dancer with whom I could appear on my own account at theatres or halls. Taking up the Era, I found that a clever young artist, Mons. Pledge, required an engagement, and the reference was to Brown's Circus at Alford. I took an early train thither, and arrived at the chief hotel in time to have breakfast, and a good old-fashioned Lincolnshire breakfast it was.

Soon after, Brown's equestrian company arrived in grand procession. The landlord came to me and said, "Splendid day for your business." Now I was an entire stranger to him, never having been in his house before. So I replied, "About as fine for your business as for mine." He said, " I beg your pardon, sir, I thought you belonged to the circus." This expression rather annoyed me, for I had not a comforter round my neck, nor long hair, nor jack boots, nor Birmingham jewellery, nor any of the other outward signs which distinguished the performers of that circus. So I pulled him up with a round turn, and said, "How dare you take me for one of those fellows?" He apologized and retired. I immediately rang the bell and required the attendance of "boots." I wrote upon a card "Captain the Hon. Adolphus Fitzhugh," and desired him to go to the post office, and see if there were any letters for that name. Of course there were none. During his absence I took the opportunity of visiting the spot where they were erecting the marquée for the circus performance. I then discovered the artist I was in quest of had left the company the previous Saturday; so my errand was fruitless so far as he was concerned. On my return to the hotel, I found that boots had telegraphed my card through the whole house. The landlord was bobbing his head, the landlady curtesying, and the waiter most obsequiously ushered me with much ceremony into a private room upstairs, thinking, I suppose, the coffee-room too common for my honourable presence. I departed, satisfied with my fare and the charges, leaving the landlord highly exalted with the idea of having entertained such a distinguished guest. But my greatness was doomed to collapse. About a year afterwards I visited Alford again, this time professionally. Apartments were taken for me at the same hotel, and a lithographed likeness of myself was exhibited in the window. So you may imagine the merry meeting of the landlord and myself, when on alighting from the carriage, he recognized me, and hat in hand conducted me into the apartment of my former grandeur. He ordered in a bottle of wine, and begged me to keep the secret, especially in that town, or he should ever after be saluted as

"Captain Adolphus." I made a promise that I would, which I have kept and shall keep to the end. As you see, his name is withheld.

From my provincial tour I returned to Hull, at the time when Z. C. Pearson, Esq., the mayor, was presenting the town with twenty-seven acres of ground to form a public park. It was a noble gift, and was presented with great ceremony. There were more than forty thousand persons present. The weather had been very rainy for some days previously, and as the land was low, flat, and undrained, you can readily believe that the tramping of forty thousand pairs of feet soon converted what was called a park into a most uncomfortable quagmire. There was to have been a review of the rifles, but that was prevented by the difficulty of manœuvering in the mud. To accommodate the juveniles there was another opening next day, to which all the charity children of the town and neighbourhood were admitted free. So the little ducks were allowed to paddle in the slush to the music of long-winded speeches from the mayor and corporation. Now it happened that an old friend of mine, George Hartley, of the Bull Inn, had given a hundred pounds towards the opening expenses, for the privilege of providing refreshments for the worthy donor, his muncipal associates, and the dear public. But I don't believe he ever saw a shilling belonging to any one connected with the affair in an official capacity. I think those who dined any where took dinners at the Railway Hotel. The second day, I must tell you, was a most lamentable failure. For with the exception of myself and half a dozen friends, about six hundred charity and workhouse children, with Sergeant Hobson and forty constables to keep seven of us in order, the park was empty. Our friend Hartley, who had expected at least ten thousand customers, and had provided accordingly an immense stock of provisions of every kind, felt

"Like one who treads alone
Some banquet hall deserted."

It was indeed a sorrowful sight. There were at least four times as many waiters as visitors who had paid for admission. So I said to George, "What are you going to do with all that good food?" He replied he didn't know; a great part must be wasted or given away. I told him if he would take a reasonable price, I would treat the multitude of little ones who were fasting in this muddy wilderness. So we came to terms for feeding the whole lot with ham, beef, tea, coffee, &c., and as one thing was exhausted to supply something else till all were fed. The refreshment saloons were at some distance from the hustings, and we had great difficulty at first in persuading the children to leave their appointed places to go to the feast I had provided. The news seemed too good to be true. However, with the assistance of my friends, I managed at last to decoy about a dozen of them away. They soon returned with full stomachs proclaiming that there was corn in Egypt. The news was buzzed round, and the next detachment consisted of about a hundred. When these returned with half-consumed sandwiches in their hands, a general stampede took place which left the learned speaker, D—— S——, Q.C. to address the police force. I stepped up just as the last of the youngsters were departing for the land of plenty, and caught this sentence, " My dear children, your worthy mayor, who has given you this park for the use of yourselves, your children, and your children's children, will prove to you what may be achieved by perseverance, sobriety, and industry. For your worthy mayor, who has made this munificent present, was once a poor boy like one of yourselves." I then stood forward and told him I thought there must be some mistake, as I was sure if the worthy mayor had ever been a poor boy, he would have been perfectly aware that poor lads are always hungry, and if they were not they soon would be. I then addressed his worship and suggested the propriety of deferring the speechifying till the children had finished their repast. He then, with the speaker's permission, said they would adjourn the meeting for an hour, which I considered very judicious, seeing there was hardly any one left to address except the guards (blue) in my rear. I made my way to the refreshment room, to superintend the commissariat of my troops, and had not been there long before a procession advanced, the leader in a red cloak trimmed with fur. He was the spokesman, and delivered to George Hartley his worship's compliments, desiring to know what was the charge for the children's refreshment. I told my friend of the *robe rouge* to give my compliments to his worship the mayor, and tell him that the children were half-fed, and all paid for before he had a thought upon the matter.

Well, his worship was a noble and spirited man, and the park proved a great blessing to the town. I would that he were now in the same position as when he made the present. It would silence the snarling of many a mean and ungrateful cur. It is too true what a great man once said: "It is loyalty to scout a falling ruler, treason to condemn a rising one." But notwithstanding my high appreciation of his work and liberality, I took the wind out of his sails that day.

He had presented the value of thousands of pounds whilst I had given but a few pounds. 'Tis true my mite was as much in proportion to my means as his largess was to his. But as the poet says,

"One touch of nature makes the whole world kin."

And I had the good-fortune to touch that chord which vibrates through all hearts. I awakened the gratitude of the children, and the sympathies of their parents and friends. On my departure from the park, I received a perfect ovation from an admiring crowd outside, while the donor of the park and his splendid retinue passed almost unheeded. His present was something that had to be made available; my treat was a reality of present profit.

A most painful incident occurred during this sojourn in England. I was playing in Hull at the Queen's Theatre, under the management of Wolfenden and Melbourne. My friend Wolfenden, from whom I received many kindnesses and the present of a very valuable diamond ring, was a noble-looking man. As large as Henry VIII., but with a heart to correspond. He could do most things well, but equestrianism was not his forte. Unfortunately he took it into his head that he could ride, and accordingly bought a horse. A party of us went out for a day in the country, and as the horse was fresh and shy I rode him out of the town, my friend taking my place in the dog-cart. Though I had been above thirty years accustomed to horses, it required all the nerve and experience I had gained to keep what is called "a true and perfect seat." I overtook the trap about two miles from Hull, and dismounted, vowing I would not ride the horse another mile if I might have him as a gift. Wolfenden was annoyed, and stepped from the dog-cart, saying, "You've all made up your minds to crab the horse; I can ride him." He mounted, when the horse immediately ran off at a terrible speed. We pursued with all haste, though we could scarcely see a dozen yards before us, owing to the dust raised by the mad gallop. At length we came in sight of something lying by the road side. The horse was gone, but poor Wolfenden remained, or rather his wreck, for his skull was fractured. He never spoke again. Our friends hastened every way, to procure surgical assistance. I was left alone with my dying friend. Luckily a poor itinerant German glazier came up, and afforded me all the assistance his better nature prompted. Down went his pack of glass, and running down to the bright beck that ran close to us, he filled his cap with water, and helped me to wash off the blood, bathe the temples, and moisten the livid lips of the wounded one. A farmer, a friend, coming up, I begged him to get a light spring cart filled with loose hay, in which we made a bed. A gentleman then passing on horseback on his way to Hull, I got him to hasten to the Infirmary, state what had occurred, and request that every thing should be ready to receive the patient. I was very much blamed for this at the time, but I will explain my reason for so acting. I then had a residence on Spring Bank, and had to pass the Infirmary daily unless I was from home. A few weeks previously Wolfenden and his partner Mr. Robert Melbourne, also deceased, had given fifty pounds to the Infirmary. One fine night, as Wolfenden and I were returning home from a friendly glass with Joseph Firth (say Old Joe), coming to the Infirmary, we paused and looked up at the lighted windows. I said, " Oh, Wolfenden, what sorrow and suffering are behind those curtains! let us be grateful that we are here in health and strength." He said, "Amen. But I consider it one of the finest institutions in Europe. If any thing were to happen to me in the shape of accident, that is the place of all others I should like to be taken to; for I feel assured I should receive all that skill can do or humanity prompt." On our arrival we backed the cart into the grand entrance, where we found a litter waiting. Our friend was conveyed to a room ready prepared. Sir H. Cooper, Dr. Gibson, and Dr. Harding were on the spot. Thus his own ideas of the Institution were realized in his case. It indeed combined the highest medical talent with the most Christian sympathy and kindness. All human aid, however, was unavailing. Within a week he slept his last sleep. At his funeral at least twenty thousand persons lined the streets, to pay their last respects to a man universally beloved. I had the melancholy satisfaction of leading his bereaved wife to the grave. The vast cemetery was crowded by a host of mourning friends. Well did he deserve that tribute. Though he and his partner are no more, I can still testify that two more liberal men as managers I never met during my career. They were the first to assist the necessitous on all occasions. For many years, independent of their private charities, they gave an annual tea to upwards of two hundred poor old women in the public gardens. The entertainment consisted of tea, music, fireworks, gymnastics, and dancing for those who could still enjoy a repetition of their youthful pleasures. But now the feast is over, the guests have departed, the lights are extinguished. Our theatre at Hull too is no more, and

> "Like the baseless fabric of a vision,
> Leaves not a wrack behind."

Soon after this I entered into partnership with Mr. James Newsome, and fitted out one of the most complete establishments ever known. We opened at the Circus, Moor Street, Birmingham, where we had a season of unflagging prosperity of nearly four months. The following spring we started on a tenting tour, with forty horses, new harness, splendid carriage, new tent by Griffin, and all the appointments of a first class equestrian troupe—not a gingerbread outside show. We made a successful tour, and returned for the winter to our old quarters in Birmingham, where we had fitted up, I have the presumption to say, the only classically decorated amphitheatre ever opened in England. During this season we produced Cinderella on a scale of splendour never before attempted—thanks to the kind assistance of Madame Newsome, who had the superintendence of the new wardrobe, &c. ; and we were well repaid for our trouble and outlay. We were favoured with the patronage and support of the Right Hon. Lord Leigh, Lord Calthorpe, Lord Exmouth, Sir John Radcliffe, &c. A week or two before we opened there was a most terrible explosion at a gun-cap factory, belonging to Mr. Purcell, in which many who had been the support of their little homes were killed or rendered incapable of work. Newsome and I gave the whole proceeds of our opening night, amounting to eighty pounds, for the benefit of their families. As we were liberally supported during the season, we gave a helping hand to many charitable institutions. My donations alone procured me a life-governorship of every charity in Birmingham.

In the centre of our colossal circus was suspended a chandelier by Defries, of London, which cost a thousand guineas. The building was draped with many thousand yards of scarlet cloth, with black velvet ornaments, and a bullion fringe a yard deep. The whole formed into festoons, supported by flying Cupids. The surrounding columns each supported a colossal piece of classic sculpture. There was no sawdust in the arena, the horses ran upon a woven fabric of cocoa-nut pile; and the centre was covered by an elegant circular carpet of chaste design.

After Newsome and I had been together for two years, we agreed to separate. So I sold off my stock in Leeds, and joined Mr. Pablo in Bristol. Here I was very kindly treated, and presented with a silver cigar-case by a number of citizens at the Two Trees Tavern, kept by Mr. Bale.

My next engagement was in old Yorkshire again. The night I opened in Wakefield, there was a man in the pit who had annoyed the company several times during the early part of the evening. It appeared he knew my name well, and perhaps he had been an early acquaintance, but I had no recollection of him whatever. At length the audience began to cry "Turn him out." "Oh," said he, "Turn him out! You just wait till old Wallett comes in; he'll let you see who'll turn me out. I tell ye, gentlemen, I know him, and he knows me, and he'd like to catch any of ye turning me out." On my appearance, I received a hearty greeting, and when the cheering subsided, my friend jumped up, and said, "That's him, that's old Wallett; now I'd like to see any of you beggars turn me out." During the confusion this speech created, I sat down upon the ring fence, close to the gallery, and said quietly to those behind me, "What's his name? Where does he come from? Give me all the information you can." So several answered at once, "Come here, I'm a neighbour of his, sit before me." I complied, and thus obtained as many prompters as I could desire. When my vociferous friend bawled out, "Dost thou know me?" I replied, "I should think I do." "What's my name, then?" "Why, they call thee Johnny Walker." "Right, my lad. What trade am I?" "Thou art a clothier." "I am, my lad. Now then, ye beggars, didn't I tell ye that he knowed me. Now, which of ye is going to turn me out?" I said, "I'm sorry to hear thou could only pay seven shillings in the pound since I saw thee last." "Eh, didst thou hear of that?" "Have you made matters up with that widow woman at the Chequers?" "Eh, didst thou hear of that and all. I told ye he knowed me, ladies and gentlemen." I rejoined, "I believe she would have married ye, John, if it hadn't been for Sal Bateson and that two-shilling-a-week job." "Nay, nay, old Wallett, that's too much." In fact, I had so many prompters, I could have told him his whole history, and they would have been proud and happy in the mischief-making. But the last blow was too heavy for him, and he left precipitately, saying, "Nay, then, if I've walked all the way from Silcoates, and paid a shilling to have all my private matters made public, it's time to shut up." His departure was signalized by the loudest cheers that ever saluted him or any of his family, I should imagine. This impromptu performance was by far the most diverting part of the evening's entertainment.

The theatre opened on the same night, in opposition to our circus, and, in playbill parlance, announced a powerful and talented company, selected from all the Theatres Royal that ever were, and some that never were. I had not time to pay them a visit, my own duties preventing me. But the Wakefield paper, on the following Saturday, supplied me with all the information required. The paragraph ran thus:—

"The Theatre Royal opened on Monday night, under new management. During the recess it has been properly cleansed, and we might say beautified. There is a brilliant light, the scenery is good, and the wardrobe excellent. An efficient orchestra discoursed sweet music. In fact, altogether it would have constituted a first class entertainment if there had been no acting."

Alas, poor Yorick!

I next engaged John Delavanti and his talented family as riders, rope dancers, and acrobats. Our performances at every place were crowned with great success. John Wilton Hall acted as my agent. He was a great traveller and a wonderful man. It was he who took Jenny Lind on her American tour; also Anderson the Wizard, Gustavus Brooke, Sir William Don, and others on their professional journeys round the world. He was likewise my agent when I first went to the United States. Alas! he is now at rest in an Australian grave.

During our tour we appeared at Drury Lane Theatre, then under the management of Mr. Spence Stokes, an American. The principal attraction was the superlative riding of a young lady called Ella, who performed feats of graceful daring never before attempted by any equestrienne. She was idolized by the young swells frequenting the theatres, and created quite a furore. But she proved to be "a mockery, a delusion, and a snare." For, shortly after this, when Ella was performing in a cirque in Germany, with princes and dukes for suitors, being serenaded every night, and receiving valuable presents of diamond bracelets, rings, &c., it was all at once discovered by convincing evidence that the charming Ella was no woman at all, but a human of the masculine gender. The deception had been well kept up, for I had known Ella upwards of seven years, and never had the slightest suspicion of her sexual deception, although I was acquainted with her mother in New Orleans. As soon as the trick was exposed, the news spread like wildfire. Fellows who had kissed her hand with rapture, and made her costly presents, were rushing about like madmen, with pistols and swords, to take the life of the male syren. With the aid of some ingenuity and a clever diguise, however, an escape was made. And the last time I saw the fascinating Ella, he was accompanied by a cheerful and amiable wife, and was the father of two lovely children. The exposure must have caused a blush on the faces of many honest females in Great Britain and America, for he had for years dressed with actresses in their rooms, and been received into private families on terms of the greatest intimacy with the ladies, as perfectly unsuspected as Don Juan in the harem. This made the imposition cruel; taking in the public might be pardoned.

CHAPTER X.

"Say, shall we write you up, or cut you down."—The Critic.

FROM the earliest time of my stepping into the sawdust, the London press has been constantly complaining of the ignorance of equestrian clowns, and the threadbare poverty of their venerable jokes. You would have imagined they would have hailed with delight any step towards the realization of their conception of what clowns should be. But my humble efforts to elevate the character were never appreciated by them. They cut me up right and left. Even the great "Thunderer" joined in the noisy cabal, and launched his bolts at my devoted head. I am not such a "fool" as to answer my brother according to his folly, so I made no reply. Not even noticing the strictures of the industrious author of "The History of Court Fools." I appeal to the public *vivâ voce*, and they have always supported me: I am content. I remember some of the opinions expressed at the time. My costume, they said, was not correct for a jester, though it was copied from an illuminated drawing in the British Museum, which, in my ignorance, I considered to be good authority. Others said that the speechifying was not in character, that a clown should have heels but no tongue: ignoring altogether

Shakespere's description of Yorick, his "flashes of merriment that were wont to set the table on a roar." He was remembered for his tongue and not for his heels; his wit, and not his grimace; his loving heart, and not his fantastic tricks. For Hamlet not only admired him as a jester, but loved him as a friend. Does he not say,

"Here hung those lips that I have kissed I know not how oft."

However, like the ass in the fable, I patiently bore my burden. For I felt that a time would come when I might wear my heart upon my sleeve. So I bided that time. Meanwhile, though I was little known to the great world of London, I was nightly received with every demonstration of approbation. At length the great evening of the Derby Day came. I knew that hundreds of my horsey country cousins, who would come up to see the race, would attend the theatre, and that before such a jury I should be sure of a fair trial. I was not deceived. During the evening, in a short lecture upon the fools of olden time, coming down to modern days, I convinced my audience—perhaps, under the circumstances, a partial one—that I was right, and my detractors egregiously, if not wilfully, wrong. Hearty ringing cheers, which made old Drury echo again and again, were given to confirm the verdict. I thanked my friends sincerely, and promised that whatever ability I might possess should always be at the command of the dear delightful public that honourably pays for its gratification; and that, with the exception of rendering the courtesy due to every man, I would never be at any pains to gratify the free list.

Leaving Drury Lane, I went to the Circus, Edinburgh. I

was welcomed by a house crowded in every part, and managed on the opening night to get up quite an exciting scene. I told them I had been very much disappointed, and my feelings were much hurt by what I had seen on my arrival. For I had always had a great love for old Scotland, my grandfather being a Scotchman, born in Dalmillington, Ayrshire, the land of Burns. I had cherished their glorious memories—the prowess of Wallace, the noble deeds of Bruce, the genius of Allan Ramsay, Ferguson, Walter Scott, and above all, the immortal Burns. But, oh, how altered now! "Stands Scotland where it did?" A nation that had fought for ages for its independence, for civil and religious liberty—that gave birth to the self-sacrificing Covenanters, and a noble army of statesmen and warriors—that had detested slavery in every form—to imagine that such a people had become the most abject of slaves themselves! You may conceive the effect this speech had upon a high-minded patriotic audience. For a time they listened in silence, but shortly began to show signs of uneasiness, followed by rising displeasure. I proceeded, and told them that with such an exalted idea as I had of the genius, valour, and unflagging energy of the whole nation, I was shocked to find that things were worse in Edinburgh than even in the slave states of America, where the poorest nigger would sell for at least two hundred pounds. Marked disapprobation. "Yes," I continued, "you may more easily conceive than describe my feelings, when stepping out of the railway train I was offered a 'SCOTSMAN' for one penny!" Then came such a burst of applause as I have seldom heard. I said, "But this is not the worst, though in Edinburgh you can actually buy a Scotsman for a penny, matters are still worse in Glasgow, where you may purchase a 'CITIZEN' for a halfpenny." The immediate effect of these puns convinced me that Sydney Smith was not altogether right when he said that it required a surgical operation to get a joke into a Scotchman. And I must here honestly confess that in all my wanderings I have never met with a keener appreciation of my jokes and humble efforts to please, nor have ever been better supported than during my visits to the "land of cakes." I tender my gratitude in the following stanzas:—

> Scotland is the home of beauty,
>   Scotland is the land of song:
> Scotland's sons will do their duty;
>   May she hold her honours long.
> May his arm fall from his shoulder,
>   Who would ere refuse to raise
> A sword to guard her ancient freedom,
>   A pen to chronicle her praise.

My next visit was to "bonnie Dundee." It appeared that previous to my arrival a company had been performing at low prices. But on the strength of my arrival they doubled the admission money. Notwithstanding the increased prices the house was nightly crowded. The managers had arranged with the authorities and gentry of the neighbourhood to give an entire night's receipts in aid of a fund for the building of a life boat. The event was to come off the week after my engagement. But as I had proved so attractive during my week, a deputation waited upon me to secure my services for that special evening. As I had made no arrangements for that time, of course I gladly consented to assist in so good a cause. They offered me a handsome gratuity, which I respectfully declined. Only I stipulated that as the circus was not very large and the sum required was, and as the committee of management could sell many more tickets than could fill the place without the ordinary public support, the prices of admission should be again doubled, to which they assented. It was a great success; the house was crowded to suffocation, and a handsome sum realized.

A night previous to the life boat benefit, I happened to pop into a house to get a glass of toddy, and while standing at the counter, I overheard the following dialogue between a labouring man and the landlady. She said to him, "Are you going to the circus to-morrow night, Mr. McGregor?" He very gruffly replied, "No, Mrs. McFaddyan." "Why, you used to go there every night at one time, Mac." "Aye, then it was only thruppence to the gallery, and a puir body could enjoy himself for twa hoors; but this Wollatt comes, and its saxpence now; and wha's Wollatt? Yes, I say, Mistress McFaddyan, wha's Wollatt, I'd like to ken? Wollatt, Wollatt, the plague take Wollatt! But that's no the worst, Mistress McFaddyan; for I see by the bulls that they've raised the prices again. For first it was thruppence, then saxpence, and to-morrow night it'll be a shilling, and if that Wollatt stays another week, it'll be half a croon, Mrs. McFaddyan." Such are the drawbacks of popularity.

After leaving Scotland, I took a tour through Ireland, but was obliged to return home by severe illness, which culminated in erysipelas in the head. For some time my life was despaired of; but, thanks to skilful doctoring and the untiring nursing of my dear wife, I was spared for a little longer. My doctor advised a change of air as soon as it was possible for me to travel. Just at this critical period, I received a letter from my old friend Ned Derious in America, offering me an engagement for two months in Philadelphia, for the opening of a new amphitheatre under the management of Mr. Fox. Here was a grand opportunity for a "change of air" and climate. I was still confined to bed; but on my doctor's next visit, I told him I had made up my mind to go to America on the following Saturday. He looked at me with astonishment, and, on going down stairs, he broke the news to my wife as gently as possible, telling her that my disease had taken a very bad turn, and what he had long feared had come to pass, my mind had become affected. My wife, who had observed no unusual indications of insanity, inquired what were the alarming symptoms. He replied, "He has just told me he is going to start for America next Saturday. Don't let me alarm you, but it will be a great miracle if he is not dead by that time." She burst out laughing, saying, "Oh, is that all? There's not much danger. As you recommended change of air and scene, Mr. Wallett having received a most tempting offer, we have made up our minds to go at once." And sure enough we did. I was, however, so weak and still afflicted, that I had to have a bed made up in the railway carriage. But, under the blessing of God, I believe the journey was the means of my perfect cure, and the renewing of the lease of my life.

We were to have had a compartment to ourselves, but the train was so crowded that the guard begged we would accommodate two ladies. The elder of these inquired what was the matter with me. When told it was the erysipelas in my head, she said that her husband had suffered for months from the same complaint, and had had several doctors, but received very little benefit from their treatment. But an old woman visiting them, said there was but one cure, that was to apply cloths dipped in the strongest whiskey that could be obtained. On my arrival at Liverpool I tried the experiment. The landlord of the Commercial Hotel, a worthy old friend of mine, drew me some from the cellar before it had been baptized. I must own I had some misgivings, anticipating great suffering from the application of such powerful spirit to the terrible irritation. So I applied it very cautiously at first. But feeling no pain I persevered, and to my surprise, instead of increasing the inflammation, in a few minutes I was free from suffering. In two hours my head was as cool as if I had never had this affliction. I continued the application of whiskey lotion, assisting its operation by small and judicious internal doses. I make this remedy public as "an act of gratitude," as some quack advertisements say, and strongly recommend it to similar sufferers. But I was in such a prostrate condition that it required four men to help me on board the ship in which I was going out to amuse the American public.

It happened on my way to Ireland to play my tour there, that when I arrived at Crewe, stepping out of the carriage who should I meet but Gustavus Brooke. While conversing with him, Mr. Toole, the comedian, came up. Then we compared notes, where we were going to. "I'm going to Dublin. And you?" "To Dublin." "And you?" "To Dublin." We found we were all to open on the same night. Toole at the Theatre Royal, Brooke at the Queen's Theatre, and Wallett at the Circus. We had a jolly time en route. One day I received a note from Brooke, stating that he had made many endeavours to find me, but discovered I was as inaccessible as a prime-minister. At length we met, and I found his object was to let me know that he was about to sail for Australia, and wished me to go with him, promising that as I had to go to the United States, he would accompany me there *via* Australia. Fortunately for me I did not consent, or I should most likely have shared his sad fate in the "London." However, though not with him, I had a fair sample of the same storm. For I left Liverpool on the same day that his vessel sailed from London. I went in the steamship City of Baltimore, Capt. McQuigan, than whom a more careful commander or better sailor never trod the quarter-deck. I had crossed the Atlantic several times with him, even so far back as when he was only a second officer in the same Inman line. He was a generous son of the Emerald Isle, and had all the heart and a good share of the wit which distinguish most of his compatriots. He was a believer in the good or ill luck of certain regular passengers. I recollect him saying to me as we were about leaving port, when one came on board, "By jabers, there's that Mr. Fielding going out with us. We'll have a storm that'll blow the sticks out of her," meaning the masts, though unluckily for his metaphor these were made of iron. Sure enough we had such a storm. A gale blew right in our teeth as we went down the channel. However we made Queenstown in safety, where we cast anchor for the night. At daylight next morning the coast in sight was strewn with wrecks. There were at least five or six within a short distance. Nothing daunted, we weighed anchor, and ran out of the bay, where we were at least two hours before we could get the pilot into his boat to return. His last words were, "God be wid yous, boys, I wouldn't be wid you for half auld Ireland and all Americky."

Our boilers were so faulty that the valves were fixed so that we could not work to above half the pressure the engines required. It blew a perfect hurricane from the westward the whole of the voyage. We lost our figure head, and had much damage done to the ship. Our voyage was so long that we had eventually to fall back upon a reserve bunk of coal that had been in the vessel since her first voyage. The gas in this coal was so exhausted that we could scarcely produce steam enough to keep the engines in motion and the ship under steerage way. At last we reached New York, after being nineteen days out. We did much better than many of the ships which left at the same time, but were compelled to run for Halifax and other Atlantic ports to replenish their supply of coal.

CHAPTER XI.

"Life is at most a meeting and a parting."—Gerald Massey.

ON landing at New York, I found that my friend Derious from Philadelphia, and a host of old friends belonging to the Isle of Manhattan, had come to meet me. After a day's rest, and being feasted and fêted at my hotel, the Washington, and serenaded by Dodsworth's band, I started for the Quaker City. There I found a carriage and four in waiting, with military companies, fire brigades and hose companies, two military bands, and several private carriages of the authorities and principal citizens, to welcome my arrival. When I issued from the railway station there could not be less than thirty thousand people within sight, and all the way from the Kensington depôt to the Continental Hotel, a distance of nearly two miles, the shops were closed, the streets lined with spectators, and the windows filled with ladies, who saluted me with their handkerchiefs. In fact, it was such a welcome as was never accorded to any actor or performer in the world's history. A more flattering reception could not have been given had it been the arrival of our beloved Queen, instead of a poor unassuming clown. I commenced my engagement a week afterwards, and the demonstrations on my appearance amounted to a furore. The following notice of this event appeared in the "Philadelphian" of that date, 4th February, 1866:—

"New American Theatre and National Circus.—The reception of Mr. Wallett, the celebrated English clown, on Monday Evening, was one well calculated to embarrass even the recipient, accustomed as he is to the public's applause. . . . . "

It was about this time that I first heard of the unhappy fate of my lamented friend Gustavus V. Brooke; and felt a thrill of gratitude that I had not accepted his invitation to accompany him. I have, however, had many nearer escapes than this. On one occasion, when I left a company in Newcastle, a vessel, the Northern Yacht, was to sail for Hull, whither I was bound, on Sunday morning at four o'clock, a very untimely hour. So on Saturday I asked the captain if he would be kind enough to allow me to come on board that evening. I found that he was a fellow-townsman. He not only granted my request, but invited us to dine and pass the day with him on the ship Then, as he said, we could go to bed at our usual time, and get up to breakfast out at sea. We accordingly went on board. About ten o'clock my wife retired with our only child, and the captain and I remained on deck to smoke our cigars. While the vessel was riding in the stream we were hailed from the shore. The captain sent a boat, and James and Thomas Cooke returned in it. I had had a misunderstanding with them, which they then settled, and offered me an advance of salary to rejoin them. My wife, who was a high-minded woman, strongly objected at first; but when she saw me resolved, and beginning to pack up my apparel, she followed suit. It was within an hour of the time of sailing when we left the ship. She quitted the Tyne, but not a plank was found, nor a soul saved to tell the story of her foundering.

On another occasion, when I resided in London, I had to go to Birmingham to fulfil an engagement. Being a fine summer's day, my wife and a visitor rode down with me to the station, in order to have a pleasant walk home again. My attention being taken up by the ladies, I was not so attentive in looking after my luggage as is my wont. When the bulk of it was packed on the roof of the railway carriage at Euston Square, and I had taken my seat, I discovered that my carpet bag was missing. I rushed back into the yard, and fortunately found our cab with my bag inside. Returning to the platform I found the train in motion. I endeavoured to enter the carriage, but was prevented by the porters and police. The train proceeded in safety till it reached Rugby, where, by some mistake of a pointsman, it came into collision with a coal train standing on a siding. My trunks were literally smashed to pieces; so much so that I had to go into the town of Rugby to procure wrappering and cords to bundle up my wardrobe. The carriage in which I had taken my place was broken up, and all its occupants injured.

Again, during my engagement at the St. Charles's, New Orleans, Mrs. Wallett, who had been on a visit to Europe, arriving at Philadelphia on her return, and finding I had gone south, without communicating with me started off with nurse and child to join me in New Orleans. I had not the slightest idea she had left England. One day, while standing in the bar room of the Gem, conversing with Dr. Brady, a telegram was brought informing me that my family had arrived in the steamboat Highland Mary at the entrepôt for the port of New Orleans. I mentioned this to the doctor, who told me that the vessel would probably be detained there some hours, as they would have to deliver the cattle, wash the decks, and give the ship a regular cleansing, before she would be allowed to land her passengers at the Levee. He kindly placed his carriage and pair at my disposal to fetch my family from the vessel at once; of which favour I of course gladly availed myself. Driving down, I found them quite well, and enjoyed one of those happy meetings which brighten the pathway of life. We joyously jogged our way home, where a good dinner awaited us which I had prudently ordered before starting. While with appetites sharpened by the drive and the zest of pleasurable associations we made a hearty meal, we little dreamt of the scene of devastation from which we had just escaped. But before the cloth was removed I heard the news-boys crying in the street—"Third edition of the Picayune—terrible explosion—one hundred and thirty lives lost—bursting of boilers of the Highland Mary!" It appeared that after we left every thing had proceeded as usual on board till orders were given to go ahead. Then the first stroke of the engines, I suppose, by injecting a volume of cold water into the heated boilers caused the fatal catastrophe. Our hearts, so full of joy a few moments ago, were now filled with gratitude, and with bowed head and bent knee, we offered up a prayer of thanksgiving for this almost miraculous escape.

I could narrate many minor escapes from accident by coaches upsetting, poles breaking, runaway horses, shipwrecks, &c.; for I have had a fair share of the disasters, as well as a full share of the blessings of an ordinary human life. Here is one of my slices of luck. Previous to leaving England on my last voyage I had appeared with Mr. Hengler in the Cirque Varieté, Hull. On my way home I lost from my luggage a small black bag at the Midland Railway Station, Nottingham. It contained a gold watch and chain, three diamond rings, valuable bracelets, and about eighty pounds in cash. The officials were very obliging, telegraphing to all stations, and making every inquiry possible. I placed the matter in the hands of the chief constable at Nottingham, and detectives were employed, as it was generally believed the bag had been stolen. However, all endeavours proved fruitless, and a few months after we left for our transatlantic visit. During the last week of my engagement at Philadelphia, I received a letter from my father-in-law, Mr. John Farmer, residing in Nottingham, and the first lines that gladdened my eyesight, were "Huzza, huzza, huzza! the bag, the bag, the bag is found!" Yes, the bag had indeed been found, with all its valuable contents intact. It had turned up at some small station, and been sent on to Derby. It was not directed; let this be a caution to all travellers. There was no difficulty however in its identification; for on opening it the first object presented was a portrait of myself, that had been given to me by my dear mother during my last visit to Hull. The precious bag was forwarded to my residence at Beeston by one from whom I had received many favours, and to whom half the travelling community are under many obligations. Peace be with him. A tear for his untimely end. Poor George Rickman!

My engagement at Philadelphia was satisfactory to myself and profitable to the management, although there were many competitors for the favour of the public. The theatres were all open; we had also an opposition circus, a large menagerie, skating on the ice by torchlight, concerts, balls, and masquerades. You may imagine the attraction of the latter, held at the Academy of Music, when it was quite a common occurrence to have from four to six thousand persons present. I attended one myself, which was given by Professor Risley and a society with which he was connected, when upwards of eight thousand were admitted during the evening. Besides these great attractions, of course there was a legion of "Original Christy Minstrels." In fact nearly as many as inundate this country just now. The original Christy band consisted of E. P. Christy and six others. There was certainly another performer in the band who went by the name of George Christy, but that was only an assumed name. Thus I never could understand how the five thousand "Original Christy Minstrels" I have met in various parts of the world could have sprung from one Christy and six artistes. Christy himself could not be called an artiste, for he could not play any instrument, and with the exception of myself was the worst singer that ever offended a musical ear. And if the original Christy had not ended a very doubtful career by committing suicide, which makes me unwilling to speak unkindly of the dead, I might be tempted to give a biographical sketch of his career that would be anything but flattering to the lowest troupes that are daily blackguarding each other in their advertisements, and squabbling for the honour of being his true descendants.

My eight weeks' engagement at Philadelphia terminated, having been one round of festivities, parties, and complimentary benefits. I was the recipient of several valuable mementoes of old friendships renewed, though but for a brief period. I commenced successfully and finished triumphantly. On the last night of my appearance Mrs. Wallett was presented with two sets of valuable jewellery; one by Mrs. George Russell, the other by Mrs. Earnshaw. The proprietors, Messrs. Fox and Earnshaw, gave me a large silver vase, bearing the following inscription, " From Robert Fox, American Theatre, Philadelphia, to W. F. Wallett," and a testimonial of their appreciation of my services.

I had several offers to remain in America; but, as you may remember, I left England during a dangerous illness, and very suddenly. So I was desirous of returning, to put my affairs in order. Therefore, with many thanks to the public, sincere gratitude to my patrons, and a manly tear at parting with my personal friends, I bade adieu to the City of Brotherly Love, several of my old chums accompanying me to New York to be present at my embarkation for Europe.

On St. Patrick's Day in the morning, I sailed in the steam ship City of New York, Captain Robert Leitch, along with a noble fleet of screw steamers bound for Glasgow, Liverpool, Hamburg, Havre, &c. And though we were the last ship to leave port, before dark we had overhauled all but one of our convoys. The next morning at day-break the whole fleet was so far astern as to be out of sight. Events proved that Captain McQuigan was no prophet, and our friend Fielding no Jonah; for though he was one of my fellow passengers, we had a glorious run, and the wind didn't "blow the sticks out of her." However, "the course of true love never yet ran smooth," neither did our ship's. As we arrived at the Sand Banks, almost within sight of Liverpool, in time to be too late. There was just water enough to prevent our crossing. So for six or eight hours we had the gratification of witnessing with what ease and precision a ship of her size could be managed. During this time she was kept running at about half speed, describing circles, figures of eight, and all manner of fantastic diagrams, beautiful to behold for those who had no desire for home. I was not one of that number. They say "time and tide wait for no man"; but we had lots of men and ladies too waiting for the tide. At length the tide in our affairs was taken at the flood, and she steamed nobly up the Mersey. It was a noble sight, for it happened to be the great sailing day of transatlantic steamers. So on our upward course we had the goodly view of a fleet of gallant ships of every size, shape, and rig. It was near dusk when we landed, and I must in justice pay a compliment to the officers of the Custom House for their excellent arrangements. Also to the officers and crew of the ship for their alacrity in landing the baggage. So well was the business conducted that, although we had a large number of passengers, every thing was passed through and carried away to our comfortable hotels before eight o'clock. At least I did not hear of a single detention.

We arrived in good health and spirits at my old quarters, the Commercial Hotel, Dale Street, which I had quitted four months back more dead than alive. So bad in fact that an old friend, on the night previous to my departure for the States, jocosely observed that he thought me very ungrateful indeed, after the many years that I had been so well supported in Liverpool, that I didn't remain there to give the undertakers a job, instead of preventing a large and effective funeral by having my poor old body thrown to the fishes. About nine o'clock the Old Bar Company assembled in force, from whom I received many kind congratulations on my improved looks and health. For they had all made up their minds that the last time they saw me would indeed be the last. But, thank Providence, the end is not yet.

Early next morning I was on my way to my home at Beeston, Nottinghamshire, where I found all right, including the long missing bag. After a brief rest I paid a visit to my honoured parents, one of whom I have since lost. I then took a short tour to the principal towns of England and Scotland, concluding my trip with an engagement at Messrs. Pinder's Circus, Huddersfield. I almost consider Huddersfield and its neighbourhood as my home, as I have visited it for many years, and as it were grown up with the town and its inhabitants.

One day I took a drive out a few miles to Holmfirth, a little place connected to me by many pleasant associations. It may be remembered that some years ago a terrible accident occurred here through the bursting of immense reservoirs, when a mighty flood of waters swept through the most beautiful valley of industry in the world, spreading death and desolation in its course. It was so long ago that it scarcely lived in my recollection at the moment, but was recalled to mind by overhearing a conversation going on at the other side of the room of the tavern in which I was seated. One man said to another,

"I'm sure that's him." The other replied, "No, it cannot be him, he is a very old man now, or he must be dead." The first speaker insisted it was me, or he had never seen me in his life. Ultimately they laid a wager, and came to me to decide it. "Is your name Mr. Wallett?" "It is." "There," said he triumphantly, "I told you so; I knew I couldn't be mistaken, although it is such a time since I saw him last. Come, old friend, you must join us in a glass for old time's sake. Eh, what an age it seems since I saw you. I've never seen you since the flood!" I thought he was having a bit of a banter with me, so I replied, "Oh, aye, I recollect when we used to smoke our pipes together in the ark." But he laughingly explained, "No, no, I don't mean that flood, I mean our own Holmfirth flood."

It was now time for me to depart, so I turned my horses' heads homewards, as it was likely to be a busy night at Huddersfield. This has always been the case upon my visits, and the present was no exception to the rule. For besides having a bumper benefit, the proprietors presented me with a silver claret jug, bearing this inscription: "Presented to Wm. F. Wallett, Esq. (sans rival) by Messrs. Pinder, as a token of esteem and acknowledgment of the Artiste, on his attaining the fortieth year of his professional career, Jan. 1868."

CHAPTER XII.

"The noblest study of mankind is man."—*Pope.*

I SAID in the Introduction that this book is a collection of disjointed incidents, the truth of which description you will long since have discovered. I here gather up a few waifs and strays, to complete the packing of my wallett.

I have devoted a considerable part of my life to the study of man, not overlooking the virtues and beauties of women. It has been my practice on starting on a long voyage, whenever possible to be on board in good time, to enjoy an hour of such study in scanning the face, dress, and general appearance of each passenger as he came on deck, and thus judge his characteristic talents and temper, and with very few exceptions I have been able rightly to select the persons with whom I could fraternize for the time. It must be understood that the saloon of a steamer, with over a hundred passengers is a perfect epitome of the outside world. Though like that world, they are composed of very different atoms on their arrival on board, yet all will be shortly sorted and arranged by the operation of the laws of affinity. Separate the first day, before the end of the third congregations are formed. Here a little knot of, say twelve persons, of a religious turn of mind and sober thoughts will be found coalesced and forming a party, there another of votaries of the polite arts, there another of smokers and drinkers; but the largest party will be formed of those who find pleasure in general conversation and amusing anecdote, a cheerful song, and a night-cap the last thing, except "We won't go home till morning." Then you are sure to have a small party of card-players and gamblers. Another of those who never have a book out of their hands unless when it has to give place to a knife and fork. Then you have a little coterie of men of high intellects and scholarly acquirements, who pass all the day and part of the night in admiring the mighty wonders of the great deep, and measuring with instructed eyes the heavenly arch above spanning from the waters to the waters. Also you have a number too lazy to drink, play at cards, or come on deck to view the beauties of creation, but remain rotting in bed the whole voyage. This remark does not apply to the sea-sick; but a little anecdote will illustrate my meaning. The captain's boy or private steward generally conveys the food from the captain's table to the stewardess in bad weather, receiving from her the orders for what is required by those under her care. I overheard this conversation between the captain and his steward. "Roast beef, sir, please." The captain placed on the plate enough for my dinner. He then inquired, "Is this for a lady, boy?" "Yes, sir." He then cut a little more. "Is she a sick lady, boy?" "Yes, sir." About two ounces more. "Is the lady very sick, boy?" "Oh, very indeed." The helping was then completed by a copious supply of fat. "That'll do, boy."

On one particular voyage, when we had, as usual, every variety of character, contents and non-contents, bashful and bold, "from grave to gay, from lively to severe," the heterogeneous crowd representing in miniature the world, my skill in physiognomy was altogether at fault. My attention was especially directed to a young fellow the very picture of a fop. With his high-crowned Kossuth hat and feather, a snuff-coloured overcoat, with large pearl buttons the size of their parent oyster shells, spotless lavender gloves, thin delicate cane with which he amused himself with beating off imaginary dust from his well brushed pantaloons, from which peered out a pair of patent leather boots of most diminutive size. I thought of having some fun with my exquisite friend, and selected him as the target for my shafts of ridicule during the voyage. They never provide a hot dinner going down Channel, but a cold collation with abundance of all the real substantials of the table. The passengers are not properly arranged by numbers at this meal, according to their berths, until the second day, so they seat themselves as they please. I happened to place myself opposite to my intended victim, who ate his luncheon with his lavender kid gloves on, and was helped to plate after plate, scarcely eating a mouthful from any. I had made up my mind to christen him "Brown Buttons, Esq." His plate was again changed, when I quietly remarked to him, "You'll excuse me, sir, but you appear to me to be taking infinite trouble and pains to lay in a very choice assortment of food. Are you aware, that at the best of times there is only half-an-inch of iron plating between you and eternity? Has it ever struck you that in less than twenty-four hours you may be keeping a restaurant in your bowels for the accommodation of shrimps?" He gave a hearty laugh, and said, "I'll be hanged if I don't think you're right, sir. I'm very happy to have found some one to speak to." He immediately handed me his champagne bottle across the table, and from that moment we fraternized. He proved to be a Lieutenant Thompson, going out to Canada to join one of Her Majesty's regiments there, and a finer fellow or more genial companion I never had the good fortune to stumble over. He was a good musician, and played extremely well upon his guitar, which was decorated, to suit his own effeminate taste, with about a yard and a half of broad blue ribbon, with a large bow at each end. Perhaps it was the gift of some dear sister, for he was one of those affable kind dispositions, the result of association with sisters and lady friends, who always exercise a wonderful influence in the formation of the manners of a true gentleman.

During the voyage, one of the engineers, while lubricating the machinery in motion, was most horribly crushed. My friend then proposed that we should give a concert for the benefit of the injured man. Now my agent, John Wilton Hall, played on the concertina, and we found a man among the steerage passengers who performed upon the violin. I improvised a tambourine to complete a quartette. We thus formed another set of "Original Christy Minstrels." For the gentleman whom I thought to be a simpleton, and knew to be a dandy, in the cause of charity and humanity actually blacked his face with the rest of us, to carry out his noble project. We had the saloon crowded; the cabin passengers heartily responding to our call for aid. Our success was so great that we received a deputation from the five hundred intermediate and steerage passengers, to repeat our entertainment the following evening. The weather being fine, we gave our performance on the quarter deck, with seats on the main deck, converting it into a regular theatre, with pit, boxes, and gallery; the sailors acting as special constables to keep the gods in order. This concert realized about twenty-two pounds, and the two together enabled us to give a handsome sum to the unhappy sufferer.

I never saw my friend again after we landed. But, after the battle of the Alma, where, as Captain Thompson, he greatly distinguished himself, he returned to Hull. He met with hearty greetings on landing, as one who deserved well of his country. Being drawn through the streets in open carriage in wet and boisterous weather, standing up without his hat to return the salutations given him, he caught a severe cold, and was buried on the following Sunday, young in years, but full of honours.

Having travelled the world far and wide, over hill and dale, from torrid to frigid zone; having taken train oil with the Esquimaux, santa cruz with the Spaniards, catawba with the Western people, usqueba with the Irish, toddy with the Scotch; having wandered in such sickly countries that the towns were as well known by the names of their diseases as by their proper names; having associated with men of all sorts, of all countries, languages, complexions, and degrees; you must admit that after such extensive travels and experiences I ought to know something. In fact, I had arrived at that opinion myself. But this pleasing delusion was suddenly dissipated from my mind by a mere accident. One night I discovered that my nursery chimney was on fire, spreading dismay among the household. You must understand that I live in a lone house, with little water at hand, and no suitable assistance within half-a-mile. No time was to be lost. I snatched the children out of bed, and, having secured them, set to work in right earnest to subdue the fire. I went at it like a Trojan with pails of water and wet mops. But all in vain. I dispatched a messenger to the village, but never relaxed my endeavours. I destroyed the carpet, spoiled the furniture, defaced the walls, but still the fire raged. At length assistance came. The man rushed into the stable, got a large armful of straw and thrust it up the chimney, entirely preventing the draught. The fire was almost instantly extinguished. So with all my profound knowledge and great experience, I was taught a lesson in natural philosophy by a country chimney sweep. Alas, for the vainglory of man!

Those who have not travelled much by water can have little idea of Saturday night and Sunday at sea. Saturday evening, when the weather permits, is a festive time. The passengers are invited to the saloon, and treated with refreshments by the captain. Anecdotes and songs go round in quick succession, and the company form quite a family party, where all distinctions are lost, and general good feeling prevails. But the gem of the evening's entertainment is the toast in which all join, of "Sweethearts and wives," followed by a song and chorus—

> "But the standing toast
> That pleased me most,
> Was the wind that blows,
> And the ship that goes,
> And the lass that loves a sailor."

And if the Saturday night is thus spent in pleasant recreation, the Sunday is observed with due solemnity. It is indeed a very comely sight to see the passengers, all properly dressed, enter the saloon with calm and respectful demeanour befitting the occasion, and take their seats in proper order. Then follow the sailors in clean white trousers, blue Guernsey frocks, with bright newly-washed shining faces, though brown and sunburnt, radiant with honest openness. Hats in hand, preceded by their officers, they range themselves on seats opposite the passengers. If there is no clergyman on board, the captain reads the service. All are attentive and orderly, though sometimes their gravity is sorely tried. Such a case occurred when I was sailing in the City of Glasgow. Captain Wylie, who commanded, though a skilful navigator, had never devoted much time to scholastic acquirements, and, with the exception of his log, considered literature "one of those things that no fellah can understand." But under the coaching of Mr. Taylor, the chief engineer, he contrived to read the lesson of the day so as "to be understanded of the people." He generally had a rehearsal or two in the course of the week, so when he opened the book he was pretty well acquainted with the matter before him. On this occasion, either by accident or design, the book-marks had been misplaced, and he opened the Bible at one of the chapters of genealogy in the Chronicles. Finding himself unable to make headway through the hard names, he looked over the following chapter, and seeing more breakers ahead, and despairing of getting through in safety, he suddenly closed the book, saying, "Ye'll do very weel to-day." Then, turning to the sailors, he bawled out, "All hands on deck, there's a storm coming up!" Although we all knew there was scarcely a breath of wind or a ripple on the sea. The only calamity was, the captain had got into troubled waters.

But sometimes we had the benefit of clergy, who are not better versed in nautical than the captain in clerical lore. They frequently flounder like M.P.s attending agricultural meetings, who, in their after-dinner speeches, not confining themselves to intellectual or political facts with which they are acquainted, will display their want of knowledge by disquisitions on ploughs, harrows, turnips, and mangold wurtzel, causing many a quiet titter among their hearers better instructed in the *matter sujet*. On one voyage we were favoured with the company of the Bishop of Oregon. He kindly officiated on the Sunday, finding his see on the sea. The prayers were very impressively read, and all went off to the credit of the bishop and the edification of his congregation, until near the close of his sermon, when he unfortunately made a dive into nautical metaphor. His subject was the necessity of faith. He took up his parable, likening the world unto the ocean, and the ship to the individual man. The anchor of the ship was a good hope. He said, "When the sea roars and is troubled, and the frail bark is tempest-tossed, and the dark clouds of despair lour over it, and all hearts are dismayed, no friendly haven being within sight, then comes the glorious work of faith. And what does faith do in this trying hour? Why, into the unfathomable abyss she drops the anchor of hope." This was too much for the sailors to bear. An irrepressible old boatswain jumped up, and cried out, "No, yer honour, I'm a swap if she does." This interruption suddenly closed the service, without even the benediction. On the following Sunday I made one of a deputation to induce the bishop to preach again. He very goodnaturedly, but decidedly refused, saying, "Give my compliments to the captain, and tell him I fear I am not adapted to the service, as I dropped my anchor in the wrong place."

My life's voyage is not over, nor my professional career quite closed, but if I now drop my anchor, I trust you, dear reader, will think it is not " in the wrong place."

APPENDIX.

FROM the numerous Testimonials and Certificates presented to Mr. Wallett during his career, the following are selected, having been preserved in glazed frames. The first is from the Order of Odd Fellows, Bradford, Yorkshire.

To W. F. Wallett, Esq., Professor of Equestrianism, &c.

DEAR SIR,—It is with feelings of peculiar pleasure that we beg to present you with our undivided thanks for the kindness with which you acceded to our request, by granting that a Benefit should be given by your worthy Company in aid of the Library connected with the Odd Fellows' Literary Institution, Bradford.

At once the powers and able talents of your most excellent Company were brought into requisition, whilst your own unequalled performances were proffered with a modesty and a grace that have enkindled in our bosoms a friendship towards you only to be obliterated when memory, that delightful faculty of our nature, shall cease to perform its ordinary functions.

By your personal capabilities you have renovated the minds of many who have been borne down under the pressure of gloom and melancholy, and produced a happy cheerful smile upon the countenances, expressive of that inward joy and pleasure with which all are deeply impressed who have witnessed your performances. These are too seldom experienced by the industrious classes of our community under the trying times in which we live, and these are they who are the very bones and sinews of our nation.

It was meet, dear sir, that you should come amongst us, and that we should seek to chase away the spell that too frequently possesses the human mind. And while your visit to Bradford will be remembered by many, by none will it be more gratefully remembered than by the Independent Order of Odd Fellows' Literary Institution.

Sir, you are about to depart from our town; when you go you will carry with you our esteem and gratitude, earnestly desiring that together with your amiable lady, your valuable lives may long be preserved from accident and harm, to which your profession peculiarly exposes you.

With our sincere wishes for your future prosperity, and may all the social and domestic happiness which tends to make life sweet ever be your peaceable possession.

Accept this feeble expression of our feelings, and believe us, dear sir, with sincere gratitude,

Yours most respectfully,

JOHN RICHARD.	WILLIAM GUTHRIE.	J. T. ILLINGWORTH.
CORNELIUS HANBY.	E. S. HOLMES.	THOMAS OXTOBY.
CHARLES SIMONS.	R. HANSOM.	W. PARKINSON.
WILLIAM COATES.	JOHN HARPER.	S. SMITH.
JOHN CASSON.	S. HOLMES.	THOMAS TETLEY.
W. K. AKRAM.	JOSHUA HASTE.	C. H. TAYLOR.

JOHN GORDON, Chairman.
Bradford, Yorkshire, SAMUEL WOODHEAD, Treasurer.
July 3rd, 1849. RALPH FAWCETT, Secretary.

The two following are American Certificates.

AMERICAN DRAMATIC FUND ASSOCIATION.

This is to Certify that WILLIAM F. WALLETT, having complied with the requisitions of the Association is now a member thereof.

In testimony of which the Secretary has this day, April 21st, 1851, by order of the Board of Directors, affixed the Seal of the Corporation to this Certificate.

JOHN SEFTON, Director.
FRANCIS C. WEMYSS, Treasurer.
W. M. FLEMING, Secretary.

New York, April 21st, 1851.

MISSOURI FIRE COMPANY.

This is to certify that W. F. Wallett has served as an active Fireman in the Missouri Fire Company seven years, and is by Charter exempt from jury and military duty.

In testimony of which we have hereunto affixed the Seal of the Company, this Eleventh day of October, in the year of our Lord One Thousand Eight Hundred and Fifty One.

  Attest.   JAMES ANDERSON, President.
         R. J. DICKEY, Foreman.
         R. D. RISLEY, Secretary.

The next is from the Hammermen Society of Paisley.

PAISLEY HAMMERMEN SOCIETY.

William Frederick Wallett, Esq., of Vine Cottage, U. S.
 Entered 1853. No. 1943, P. 286.

        JOHN GILLMOUR, Præses.
        J. G. SHARPE, Collector.
        A. GIBSON, Clerk.

The following is especially valuable as proceeding from Mr. Wallett's native town.

TOWN HALL, HULL.

Town Clerk's Office, 4th Feb., 1854.

To W. F. Wallett, Esq.

DEAR SIR,—I beg to hand you the annexed Testimonial (duly certified under the seal of this office) from your fellow citizens, as showing their estimation of your rare and eminent as well as exemplary conduct.

  I am, dear sir,
   Yours very sincerely,
     LAWRENCE C. TARN,
      Assistant Town Clerk of Hull, England.

AMERICAN CIRCUS.

Complimentary Benefit, Jubilee, and Farewell to W. F. Wallett, Esq., on Friday, Feb. 3rd, 1854.

We, the undersigned Citizens of Hull, in consideration of the rare talent and exemplary conduct of our gifted townsman, W. F. Wallett, Esq., and in appreciation of those abilities which have earned for him an enviable fame in both hemispheres, who has had the high honour of being presented in person to her most Gracious Majesty the Queen of

England, besides winning golden opinions from all sorts of people, sign this testimonial in order to testify to the world that we, his fellow townsmen, wish to do him honour on his last visit to his native town, previous to his departure for America, his chosen home and land of adoption, wishing health and happiness to himself and family.

Signed,

HENRY COOPER, Mayor.
JOHN GRESHAM, Alderman.
W. B. BROWNLOW, Alderman.
W. PRIEST, JUN.
T. W. PALMER, Alderman.
THOS. ABBEY, Councillor.
WM. STEPHENSON, Councillor.
JAMES GLOVER, London Hotel.
THOS. QUILTER, Royal Hotel.
JOHN LAW, Nelson Street.
JOHN WHITE, Queen Street.
ROBT. FOSTER, JUN.,   do.
WILLIAM HARPER,   do.
JOHN SWALLOW,   do.
CHARLES YEOMANS,   do.
WILLIAM CARR,   do.
JOHN DUMAYNE,   do.
JOHN ANDERSON,   do.
EDWARD J. WATSON,   do.
GEORGE TURNMON,   do.
A. ANHOLM,   do.
H. & T. SMITH,   do.
ANN PENNACK,   do.
EDWARD CHAPMAN,   do.
GEORGE MARRIS,   do.
JOHN SYMONS,   do.
JAMES HARDING,   do.
HENRY CARROL,   do.
FELIX WOODRUFF,   do.
GEO. F. BRISTOW,   do.
SAMUEL W. KIRKE,   do.

JESSE HAMPSHIRE, Queen St.
GEORGE VICCARS,   do.
J. G. FRANKISH,   do.
GEORGE HARTLEY, Mytongate.
JOHN ATKIN,   do.
ROBERT MARRS, Queen's Hotel.
SARAH MOOR.
WM. GLEADOW, Mytongate.
JOSEPH LOFTHOUSE, Market Pl.
WILLIAM GILLETT,   do.
JOHN MORLEY,   do.
ALEXANDER BEAN,   do.
G. M. HART, Scale Lane.
J. S. HAMILTON, Lowgate.
J. H. MITCHELL,   do.
JOHN NORRIS,   do.
W. ARMSTRONG, Lowgate.
JANE DICKSON, Market Place.
DAVID BROWN,   do.
JAMES ARTHUR,   do.
ROBERT KNIGHT,   do.
P. MOSS,   do.
THOMAS NEWTON,   do.
WILLIAM BOWLBY,   do.
JOHN HOOLE,   do.
SAMUEL HALL,   do.
CLARKE BUTHIN,   do.
G. WHITAKER,   do.
J. RUSHWORTH,   do.
SPCR. HARRISON, Dock Walls.

Together with upwards of two hundred of the principal merchants and tradesmen.

APPENDIX.

The following Address received from the Mayor, the Member of Parliament, and the chief citizens of Oldham, will appropriately close this list.

To Wm. F. Wallett, Esq., of Spring Villa, Beeston, Nottingham.

We, the undersigned inhabitants of Oldham, in the county of Lancaster, being apprized by Mr. Harry Montague, the Manager for your old and esteemed friend and compeer, Pablo Fanque, Proprietor of the Mammoth Circus, of your intention shortly to retire from your professional career, venture respectfully to address you.

Through a long series of years you have with great ardour and ability devoted yourself to the public service. You have stood unrivalled in your successful efforts to please and instruct the public; you have shed a dignity upon the character of the Jester, and your efforts (in which you have blended amusement and instruction) have never degenerated into coarseness or vulgarity, but have, we believe, been characterized by a sound moral tone.

The many years actively spent by you in pursuit of your calling, entitle you to some years of retirement, rest, and seclusion. We trust you yet (as you so well deserve) may enjoy many years of quiet in the bosom of your family, and amongst your friends and immediate neighbours.

The People of Oldham have we believe in your visits supplied you with sympathetic and appreciating audiences. We know with what rapt attention your sallies of wit, humour, and satire have been received. It is with surprise that we have learned the probability that you may not again visit us. We ask you as admirers and well-wishers, that inasmuch as it has not been announced that your recent visit was a final one, you will reconsider your determination and come at least once more amongst us before you bid farewell to your present vocation.

EDMUND HARTLEY, Mayor.	JOHN PLATT, M.P.
ALDERMAN WELD.	S. R. PLATT.
JOHN STIRNDELLS.	WILLIAM BRIERLEY.
JAMES YATES, M.D.	ALDERMAN WHITTAKER.
JAMES SCHOFIELD.	J. BRIERLEY ROWLAND.
WM. WHITTAKER.	JAMES MARSHALL.
COUNCILLOR BRADLEY.	WILLIAM BLACKBURN.
JOHN REDFERN.	JAMES TWEEDALE.

GEORGE J. MURRAY.
J. D. CLEGG.
EDWARD EVANS.
W. RENNIE.
RD. DUNANS.
ROBERT ASCROFT.
JOHN POTHER.
C. E. ASCROFT.
T. SHIERS.
J. F. TWEEDALE.

W. H. ROBENSON.
WM. ASCROFT.
JOSEPH ROWLAND.
THOS. BEARD.
J. PONSONBY.
WILLIAM WILD.
THOS. HADFIELD, JUN.
CLEMENT HALL.
W. EVANS.
DANIEL BUCKLEY.

APPENDIX.

THE MATERIAL TESTIMONIALS PRESENTED TO MR. WALLETT, COMPRISE THE FOLLOWING:—

GOLDEN MEDALLION.
By Her Majesty the Queen, at Windsor Castle.

GOLDEN CROSS.
By the King of the French, at Claremont.

SILVER SNUFF BOX.
Birmingham, at the Gem Tavern, Steelhouse Lane.

DIAMOND RING.
From Sheffield, at the Amphitheatre.

SILVER SNUFF BOX.
From the Flying Horse Hotel, Nottingham.

MASSIVE VASE.
From New Orleans, given by DAN RICE, the great American Clown.

SPLENDID SERVICE OF SILVER.
From Birmingham, at Bingley Hall, J. Tonks, Esq.

DIAMOND RING.
At the Queen's Theatre, Hull, Messrs. Wolfenden and Melbourne.

SILVER CIGAR CASE.
From Bristol, Two Trees Tavern.

MARBLE BUST.
By Subscription (see Copies), Hull.

MASSIVE GOLD CUP.
Value £100, Lion and Lamb, Leicester.

MASSIVE SILVER VASE.
By R. Fox, Esq., Philadelphia.

GOLD WATCH AND MASSIVE CHAIN.
By Rowe and Smith's Circus Company at California.

GOLD HORSE AND BUCKLE.
By Rochet the Clown, at San Francisco.

SILVER CLARET JUG.
By Messrs. Pinder at Huddersfield.

"As a mark of esteem and acknowledgment of the Artiste on his attaining the 40th year of his professional career, Jan., 1868."

BEMROSE & SONS' SELECTED LIST.

Mrs. Warren's Household Manuals.

COOKERY CARDS FOR THE KITCHEN;

Being Six Large Sheets of Plain Instructions for Cooking Fish, Soups, Meat, Sauces, Vegetables, Pastry, Sweets, and Preserves. Third Edition, with additional Instructions for Making White and Brown Bread, Rolls, Cakes, &c. Price One Shilling.

"Very simple and extremely valuable."—*Christian World.*

A HOUSE AND ITS FURNISHINGS.

How to Choose a HOUSE, and Furnish it at Small Expense. Price One Shilling.

"A more useful little work of its kind has never been issued, and many young housekeepers already sighing over bad investments will wish they had gone shopping with such a guide in their hands."—*Star.*

COMFORTS FOR SMALL INCOMES.

New Edition. 25th Thousand. Price One Shilling.

"It contains a vast variety of information of every conceivable kind in regard to the management of a household, the regulation of the daily expenditure, and the art of making a little go a great way."—*John O'Groat Journal.*

COOKERY FOR £200 A YEAR,

And for Greater and Lesser Amounts of Income. Price One Shilling. [*Nearly ready.*]

21, PATERNOSTER ROW, LONDON; AND DERBY.

Bemrose & Sons' Selected List.

PHOTOGRAPHIC SCRAP ALBUM.

Twenty-four beautiful Lithographic Designs, in elegant cloth case, gilt edges, royal quarto, 24 leaves, 12/6. Forty-eight designs, 21/-.

"Messrs. Bemrose, of Paternoster-row, have just published a beautiful photographic scrap album. The work is of a large quarto size, and the spaces to receive the scraps are surrounded with elegant designs. It is splendidly bound in red and gold, and is a good presentation book."—*Court Journal.*

A NEW SERIES OF ABOVE.

Twenty-four leaves, 12/6; Forty-eight leaves, 21/-.

NUTS FOR BOYS TO CRACK.

By Rev. JOHN TODD, D.D., Pittsfield, Mass. Foolscap 8vo. Cloth neat. Price 2/6.

HINTS AND THOUGHTS FOR CHRISTIANS.

By Rev. JOHN TODD, D.D., Pittsfield, Mass. Foolscap 8vo. Cloth neat. Price 2/6.

FRET CUTTING AND PERFORATED CARVING.

With Practical Instructions, and Fifty-four Designs suitable for every description of useful and ornamental articles of Furniture and Ornament. By W. BEMROSE, Jun., Author of "Manual of Wood Carving." In Demy 4to., neatly bound in cloth, price 5s.

A MANUAL OF WOOD CARVING;

With Practical Instructions for Learners of the Art, and original and selected designs. By W. BEMROSE, Jun., with an Introduction by Llewellynn Jewitt, F.S.A. In Crown 4to., Fifth Edition, handsomely bound in cloth, price 5s.

** New Designs in Fret Cutting are being continually brought out. A Complete List of those which have already appeared will be forwarded on application.

BEMROSE'S GUIDE TO FRET CUTTING AND WOOD CARVING.

Being a List of Tools and their Uses, post free for one stamp.

21, PATERNOSTER ROW, LONDON; AND DERBY.

Bemrose & Sons' Selected List.

New Edition, Coloured Plates, Fcp. 8vo. Price 1s.
GLENNY'S FLORICULTURE;
Containing full directions for the Cultivation of all the Favourite Flowers, with their Height, Colour, Habit, and Growth. By GEORGE M. F. GLENNY.

"We have little doubt that this will be found a most useful book to those people who couple a taste for gardening with a limited space in which to exercise it, and no small share of ignorance as to the pursuit itself. The amateur gardener is here instructed in the matter of garden soils generally, what tools are requisite, and how they are to be used. He is supplied with practical suggestions as to the cultivation of flowers generally, and especially florist's flowers. Even the poor Londoner, whose horticulture is confined to a window-box is not forgotten."—*London Review.*

COOKERY FOR THE TIMES.
By BLANCHE MOORE. This Book contains well-tested and fully-described recipes, adapted for Family Dinners, &c., and is arranged on a new and simple plan, which does away with reference to an index. Crown 8vo. In one vol. or in Seven Divisions. The Divisions may be hung up like Cards, in a frame for the purpose. [*In the press.*]

ENGLISH STATESMEN FROM THE PEACE OF 1815 TO THE PASSING OF THE REFORM BILL, 1867.
By T. E. KEBBEL, M.A., Barrister-at-Law, Author of "Essays upon History and Politics." In one Volume. 8vo. Neatly bound in cloth. Price 5s.

CONTENTS.—Lord Castlereagh, Mr. Canning, Lord Palmerston, Duke of Wellington, Lord Aberdeen, Sir Robert Peel, Lord Grey, Lord Russell, Lord Derby, Mr. Gladstone, Mr. Disraeli.

"The sketches are, though professedly slight, useful, thoughtful, and interesting—more especially those which treat rather of the Statesmen representing our foreign policy between 1815 and the death of Lord Palmerston....... It is a pleasant, and in its earlier part, an instructive book. Mr. Kebbel writes well. He has studied the subject on which he writes."—*Spectator.*

"It consists of ten clever and discriminating political sketches, all of which are full of interest and exceedingly readable. Mr. Kebbel as evidently possesses a well balanced and critical mind as he does a capacity for putting his facts and thoughts into good English. The book will be welcomed and read, and deserves to be so."—*Church News.*

21, PATERNOSTER ROW, LONDON; AND DERBY.

Bemrose & Sons' Selected List.

MEMOIR OF THE LATE PARKIN JEFFCOCK,

Civil and Mining Engineer, by his brother, the Rev. J. T. JEFFCOCK, M.A., Wolstanton Vicarage, Stoke-on-Trent. With Portrait and Illustrations. Second Edition. Crown 8vo. Neat Cloth. Price 3s. 6d.

CLAUDE SPENCER; WADDLES; GERTY ROSS; AND LITTLE BLUE-COAT BOY.

Four tales in One Volume. By Mrs. F. MARSHALL WARD. Royal 16mo. Cloth neat. Price 2/6.

"Four short illustrated tales for young people, well written, with a moral purpose, and calculated to make them better and wiser."—*Churchman's Family Magazine.*

"Full of homely teaching of the right character."—*Public Opinion.*

CLAUDE SPENCER; AND WADDLES.

Two Tales in One Volume. By Mrs. F. MARSHALL WARD. Royal 16mo. Cloth neat. Price 1/6.

GERTY ROSS; AND LITTLE BLUE-COAT BOY.

Two Tales in One Volume. By Mrs. F. MARSHALL WARD. Royal 16mo. Cloth neat. Price 1/6.

THROUGH LIFE AND BEYOND; AND PAUL FENTON.

Two Tales in One Volume. By Mrs. F. MARSHALL WARD. Royal 16mo. Cloth neat. Price 1/6.

FRANK BENNET:

A Tale of the Stocking Loom and of the Lace Frame in 1811. By Mrs. C. ORLEBAR. Fcp. 8vo. Cloth elegant. 2/6.

"This is, first of all, a capital boy's story—real, unaffected, with a lively sentiment of honour and help in it: and then, also, a good story of the Luddites, and the establishment of the lace trade in Nottingham and Leicestershire."—*English Independent.*

"Mrs. Orlebar has given us a pleasant little story in 'Frank Bennet.' Its chief charm lies in the delightful little Dutch pictures it gives of home and home people. Mrs. Orlebar, however, soars higher than this, and she tells vividly and with much power a deeply interesting story. The book thoroughly deserves to be read."—*Scotsman.*

21, PATERNOSTER ROW, LONDON; AND DERBY.

BEMROSE & SONS,

WHOLESALE & MANUFACTURING STATIONERS,

GENERAL PRINTERS, LITHOGRAPHERS, ENGRAVERS, & DIE-SINKERS,

LONDON, 21, PATERNOSTER ROW, E.C.; DERBY, IRONGATE;
MATLOCK-BATH, "THE LIBRARY."

ESTIMATES GIVEN.

LETTERPRESS PRINTING,

Of every description, comprising Book-work, Magazines, Pamphlets, Colliery Rules, Joint Stock and Limited Liability Companies' Prospectuses and Forms, Wagon Tickets, Address and Advice Cards, Declaration Notes, Wagon Number Forms, &c.

CLERICAL AND PAROCHIAL PRINTING.

Sermons, Lectures, Reports, Appeals; Posters, Hand-bills, and Circulars for Special Sermons and Festivals, got up in new and original designs, as well as in the Ecclesiastical styles. Clothing Club Cards and Books, Collecting Books, Tract Covers, Admission Tickets, Church Door Notice Papers, Service Papers, &c.

BIBLES AND PRAYER BOOKS FOR THE READING DESKS AND ALTAR SERVICES SUPPLIED, BOUND IN APPROPRIATE STYLES.

WOOD ENGRAVING.

B. & S. having executed the Engravings for Scores of Churches and Schools, can confidently assure the Clergy and others who may require Wood Engravings that any orders entrusted to them will be completed in a highly satisfactory manner.

Illuminated Letters for Church and School Decorations for Christmas, Easter, and other Festivals.

Illuminations on Vellum for Presentations, either in Scrolls or Bound in chaste and appropriate styles.

LITHOGRAPHY.

Mineral Sections, plain or coloured; Architectural Drawings, Ruins, Churches, &c.; Plans of Mines, Parliamentary, Estate, and Railway Plan Sections; Receipt and Bill of Exchange Forms, Scrip and Share Certificates, Licenses, Appointments, Invoices, Advice Forms, &c.

BOOKBINDING.

To this Department especial attention is paid, and work executed in a style equal to any London House. For Binding B. & S. obtained "Honourable Mention" at the 1862 Exhibition. Estimates given for Libraries and Lots of Books.

An immense stock of Papers, comprising Browns, Cartridges, Writing and Account Book Papers, of every variety.

ORDERS EXECUTED WITH THE GREATEST PROMPTITUDE AND AT THE LOWEST PRICES.

WORKS PUBLISHED BY BEMROSE & SONS,

21, PATERNOSTER ROW, LONDON; & DERBY.

THE ARRANGED AS SAID EDITION

OF THE

BOOK OF COMMON PRAYER.

THE Arrangement of this Edition of the Book of Common Prayer removes all difficulty in following the Services, not one word of which or of the Rubrics is altered or omitted, but the whole are printed in the order in which they are read; *the Services can thus be followed with ease by those unacquainted with them*, and the use of the Book is rendered more agreeable to those already conversant with it.

The Book is paged throughout, and such is the arrangement, that the necessity of continually turning backwards and forwards is obviated. At the end of each day's Psalms, and wherever any pages require to be passed over, a reference is given by which the reader may at once pass on to the part next to be used.

The Morning and Evening Services are totally distinct, with their Psalms, Collects, &c. The Psalms for Proper Days appear in full in their proper order.

The Litany, Communion Office, Creeds, General Prayers and Thanksgivings, are placed where they are used. The Collects where repeated, as in Lent, are printed again.

Figures are used instead of numerals, and Tables of Contents, with other directions render the use of the Book of Common Prayer perfectly simple.

Prices and description of Bindings on application.

SERIALS.

The Reliquary, a Depository of Precious Relics—Legen-
dary, Biographical, and Historical; Illustrative of the Habits, Customs, and Pursuits, of our Forefathers. Edited by LLEWELLYN JEWITT, F.S.A., Member of the Archæological Institute of Great Britain and Ireland, &c. Vols. 1 to 9. Demy Octavo. Cloth, Boards. Price 11s. 6d. each. Each volume is complete in itself, and profusely Illustrated with Plates and Wood Engravings.
☞ *The Work is also Published in Quarterly Parts, Price 2s. 6d.*

The Net Cast in Many Waters. Sketches from the Lives
of Missionaries. Edited by ANNE MACKENZIE. Demy Octavo. Monthly Numbers, 1d. each. Vols. 1866, 1867, 1868, and 1869 in handsome Cloth, Price 2s. each.

The Ladies' Treasury. An Illustrated Magazine. New
Series. Edited by MRS. WARREN. Price 9d. Monthly. Royal Octavo, Cloth, gilt edges. Vols. I. and II. 4s. 6d. each; Vol. III. 10s. 6d.; Vols. IV., V. and VI. 5s. 6d.
Splendidly Illustrated with Plates and Wood Engravings.

The Naturalist's Note Book. New Series, Monthly,
Price 6d. Fourth Year of Publication. Beautifully Illustrated.

Lightning Source UK Ltd.
Milton Keynes UK
UKOW05f2108250516

275011UK00010B/220/P